FIRST WE SURF, THEN WE EAT

Recipes from a Lifetime of Surf Travel

Jim Kempton

Published by Prospect Park Books
2359 Lincoln Avenue
Altadena, California 91001
www.prospectparkbooks.com

Distributed by Consortium Book Sales & Distribution
www.cbsd.com

Library of Congress Cataloging-in-Publication Data is on file with the Library of Congress. The following is for reference only:
Kempton, Jim
First We Surf, Then We Eat: recipes from a lifetime of surf travel / by Jim Kempton — 1st ed.
     p. cm.
ISBN 978-1-945551-33-8
1. Cooking, International. 2. Cooking, Regional/Ethnic. 3. Travel, Special Interest/Sports. 4. Travel, International.

Edited by Colleen Dunn Bates
Book & cover design by Amy Inouye, Future Studio; book layout by Michelle Ingram
Cover photograph by Bill Schildge
Printed by Imago USA in China

Travel & surf photography credits

Alamy Photo: page 146
Brian Bielmann: pages 222-223
Art Brewer: pages 25, 108, 118, 128
Jeff Divine: pages 4, 9, 10, 15, 22, 30, 36, 53, 62, 82, 87, 88-89 (Catalina), 90, 103, 130-131, 142, 150, 154-155 (Todos Santos), 170, 198 (G-land), 201, 212, 218 (vendors)
Dreamstime: 108-109, 114, 116, 121, 122, 135, 234
Carlos Ferrer: page 221
Pierre Gascogne: page 52
Tom Keck: page 72
Aurelien Laborde: page 42
Russell Ord: pages 206-207
Marco Pompeo: page 80
Bill Schildge: pages 38-39, 170
Jose Schiaffino: page 218 (Chicama), 241
Brent Schlea: page 135
Tom Servais: pages 8, 13, 25-26, 29, 34, 70, 88 (surfer/boat), 94, 140, 154 (Baja), 168, 176, 177, 178, 179, 187, 192, 193, 198 (door), 202, 206, 208, 213, 224, 227
Witch's Rock Surf Camp: page 96

FIRST WE SURF, THEN WE EAT

Recipes from a Lifetime of Surf Travel

Jim Kempton

Food photography by **Bill Schildge**

Surf & travel photography by **Art Brewer, Jeff Divine & Tom Servais**

Foreword by **Steve Pezman**

Chef's foreword by **Raphael Lunetta**

Prospect Park Books

Contents

6   **The Pleasures of Knowing Jim**
Steve Pezman

8   **A Meditation on Connections**
Raphael Lunetta

10 **Surfing & Cooking:
Supreme Pleasures Impervious to Explanation**

14 **Guam, Tahiti & the Pacific**

36 **The Basque Country**

64 **California**

88 **Central America**

108 **Morocco**

130 **Hawaii**

154 **Mexico**

176 **The Caribbean**

198 **Indonesia**

218 **Peru**

242 Index

247 Acknowledgments

*Nothing like a good seafood snack after a solid surf
session. At Macaronis in Mentawais, Indonesia.*

The Pleasures of Knowing Jim

Steve Pezman

Jim Kempton in France

It's 6:30 on a Saturday evening in the hills above San Clemente. A dozen of Jim Kempton's longtime friends, including my wife, Debbee, and myself, are gathered at Michael and Leslie Davis's home at Jim's invitation to enjoy a Kempton-style evening of convivial dining. The menu consists of Moroccan dishes that Jim has recently been perfecting. Jim has been laboring over this meal for several days: the first few spent locating the more exotic ingredients, then two days of prep and cooking. Accordingly, the Davis's kitchen counters are littered with dirty mixing bowls, pots and pans, cooking utensils, and traces of ingredients. Sipping wine and catching up, we await the arrival of a leg of lamb, which is crusting on the patio grill.

On this evening his guests also include *The Surfer's Journal* photo editor and renowned surf photographer Jeff Divine and his wife, Julie; Jim's longtime friend (dating back to mid-'70s evenings at Le Steak House in Biarritz) Pierre Gascogne and his wife, Corine, and gracious Aussie photo master Ted Grambeau, who's passing through to renegotiate his gig with Quiksilver. The attendees sample various items around the dining table while Jim stands at the end, describing the origins of each dish. The meal is as richly exotic and splendid as we knew it would be.

Jim Kempton and I first met at *Surfer* magazine when I was publisher while also standing in as editor during a vacancy. He was a surf writer from San Diego who had cleverly been exporting silk-screened T-shirts with esoterically cool graphics to France. After a few months of visits, I saw that he was surf knowledgeable, worldly, and quite capable. Over the next eight years at *Surfer,* we began a surf-centric relationship encased in the common interests of riding waves and enjoying food. My enthusiasm was mostly for eating it; Jim's, perhaps even more for cooking it. He saw culinary creation as an art form.

Thus our surfing adventures—surfing a summertime south swell in Malibu with dim sum in Chinatown on the way home, attending the Eddie Aikau big-wave contest and meeting George

Downing for Oahu's best Korean barbecue, weeklong surf trips to Mexico sampling every imaginable type of taco—became enriched with culinary sidebars; on occasion it was the other way around.

When *Surfer's* parent company transferred me to oversee the company's multiple titles, management asked Jim to take over as publisher. After three years of that life-changing experience, a time when *Surfer* was quite good, Jim enlisted the owners of a successful restaurant in Tijuana to join him in opening an authentic Mexican eatery in San Clemente. The resulting Margarita's Village soon developed a cult following, drawing swarms of surfers and locals to the restaurant and bar, the latter of which gained fame by serving as the scene of several bawdy performances by certain Hall of Fame surf legends. As they always seem to do, the restaurant gig fried Jim, so finally he left to take consulting assignments from surf-industry brands that had realized that, indeed, they were lost in Kansas without the counsel of a wise surf guru like Jim. While doing that with his left hand, our friend began creating hugely imaginative celebratory dinners at his home. Each one would begin with Jim's intense interest in a certain cuisine and progress through the testing and perfecting of the recipes he'd discovered throughout his travels, and finally would come the main event.

Jim has had the charmed tendency to fall into really cool gigs. During his stint at Quiksilver, his résumé inclined them to assign him the task of coordinating and accompanying a legendary surf-world vessel, the *Indies Trader,* captained by rogue Aussie skipper Martin Daley. Jim was the onboard corporate entity. She was a trawler turned luxury, seaworthy surf explorer that carried fourteen guests plus five crew, who offered up gourmet meals, Australian wines, a full bar, evening surf films, and perfect waves, all never before so thoroughly combined and cunningly delivered. As host of a surf-exploration vessel promoting Quiksilver with an ever-changing rotation of hero surfers on board, he traveled and surfed and dined throughout Europe, Latin America, the Caribbean, and the Indian Ocean. This global multi-year adventure further nurtured his absorption of a broad spectrum of the world's culinary offerings, bolstered by his lack of queasiness—or is it an adventurous nature?—about what went in his stomach.

These days, Jim has progressed to not only collecting recipes that spike his interest and creating his own versions of them, but also writing about his unique experiences over a life of culinary and surf adventures. The book you are holding in your hands represents the tip of the proverbial iceberg. It's an invitation to a Kempton feast that you must seek.

Most admirably, throughout it all, Jim still paddles out.

Steve Pezman is the editor and publisher of The Surfer's Journal.

Jim in the zone

Chef's Foreword

Raphael Lunetta

A Meditation on Connections

The California/surf/beach lifestyle has helped create the healthy, fresh, innovative cuisine we enjoy today. For me, this goes back to the very beginning, when I lived with my aunt along the coast of France. She made old-world food—simple and pure. It fell under the Mediterranean vision: roasted vegetables, grilled meats, olive oils, fresh herbs, smashed garlic. Effortlessly healthy.

As surfing has evolved, we've come to learn about the essential connection between diet and performance. Luckily, the flavors that shaped my childhood fall in line with this way of eating. The trick is to stay innovative. You have to communicate with those around you, combine fundamental techniques with fresh ideas, and come up with something new. That's what I try to do every day. And that's what this book tries to do, too—connect two things that are really essential to our lives.

From the North Shore of Oahu to the beaches of southwest France, I've had the honor of cooking at some of the world's greatest surf destinations. There's nothing better than a day of solid surfing followed by an inspired feast with friends both old and new. Roasting chiles and slicing wahoo in Fiji, grilling local sardines in Portugal, the discovery of Swarnadwipa (a spice I first tasted on the shores of Bali)...I've been pursuing all these flavors ever since I had those experiences, and I'm currently trying to re-create them at my restaurant. Somehow or another, surfing always finds its way into my food.

When you're surfing, you're building strong personal connections. Over the years, I've come to know some of the best professional surfers in the world, and I've learned that the best way to nurture those connections is through a wonderful meal. There's an amazing feeling of appreciation when you can sit together and reflect on the day in the waves, especially when your food is coming from the same place that gave you such a special experience. In a way, that's what this book is all about.

I often start the day early, walking on the beach to check the swell, feel the wind direction, and generally absorb the conditions. It's a form of meditation, a method of connecting with nature. Starting the day that way gives me the drive and enthusiasm to come into the kitchen and paddle through a different kind of swell. My beach walk is also a constant reminder of the responsibilities we have to the ocean. The ocean never asks anything of us. It simply gives. We must try to do the same.

Raphael Lunetta is the chef/proprietor of Lunetta restaurant in Santa Monica, California.

Not many chefs can carve a wave as well as they carve a roast—
Raphael Lunetta at Cloudbreak, Tavarua, Fiji.

SURFING & COOKING:
Supreme Pleasures Impervious to Explanation

Through a lot of luck and a little quick thinking, I've been able to make a living while enjoying the three things I enjoy most: surfing, traveling, and cooking. In a certain way I've been working on this book all my life. I've had the privilege to visit forty countries, surf in most of them, and collect a lifetime of recipes and adventures.

First We Surf, Then We Eat features food from six continents, including Oceana, and the dishes range from simple to exotic. The recipes are sometimes complex but never weird. Not that I haven't experienced the weird. I've eaten *balut*—the almost-hatched embryo of a chicken or duck that's still in its shell; it's a delicacy in some regions of Asia, but in the US we're too chicken to try it. I didn't eat the beating heart of a cobra, but I've seen them do it in Bali. (Similarly, I've never surfed Jaws or Mavericks, but I have a lot of friends who have.) I'm more at home with a good Indonesian stir-fry and a head-high day at Trestles than roasting guinea pigs on hot coals in the Peruvian coastal desert or navigating thirty-foot swells in Waimea Bay.

My goal when writing this book was to offer a variety of delicious recipes that all relate to my surf travels and the surf culture. They're easy but distinctive, often featuring fresh ideas that people from around the world use to make their food—and drink—more interesting, healthier, and/or flavorful. And I wanted to have fun telling the stories of the people, places, and waves I encountered along the way. I looked for a range of recipes, from simple stuff a surfer can cook at the beach or on the road to more exotic recipes for those who like to get busy in the kitchen.

On the simple side, consider this recipe from my good friend Steve Pezman. He calls it the San Onofre Gate Guard Roast, because the aroma drives the guards crazy when you pull up to the ranger kiosk to enter San Onofre State Beach. "Take a good cut of roast as you need for optimum enjoyment, one potato per mouth, carrots, onions, and garlic. Insert garlic slivers into slits in the meat. Salt and pepper copiously. Wash veggies and wrap the roast and all veggies two times in heavy-duty aluminum foil. Tuck into a spot under the hood, in a secure part of your surf mobile's engine manifold. About an hour of driving should do it. Surf and play after arriving at your surf spot. To reheat: Idle the engine for about fifteen minutes. Open foil package and serve." No need for gourmet sauces—this simple dish

The only thing worth remarking about this shot is that Lower Trestles is glassy, overhead, lined up—and nobody is in the lineup. Except me.

is a meal in one, and totally satisfying. (Note that I have a vegetarian variation on this recipe in the California chapter, page 70.)

On the more sophisticated side, consider Mariscada, the seafood soup that's a national dish of El Salvador. The best version I've ever had is at the Las Flores surf resort, and the chef shared his recipe with me. It turns out it's really not that hard to make—it just has a lot of ingredients, all delicious. Even if you've never ridden a wave in your life, it'll bring the ocean alive at the dinner table.

In every chapter you'll find places worth visiting, people worth knowing, and surf worth traveling to enjoy. You'll be introduced to a few great restaurants where surfers hang out. And, most of all, you'll discover a lot of great recipes that perfectly suit a beach-lover's life, from smoothies to stir-fries, cocktails to crab bisque, Balinese beef satay to barracuda Caribbean-style, Peruvian quinoa-honey shrimp to Palauan papaya upside-down cake.

You'll read about narrow escapes, legendary surf stars, crazy capers, perfect waves, and healthy eating. I've included a section on superfoods and how to use them, because we surfers are a health-conscious bunch and we need our fitness-focused foods. I made sure to incorporate a superfood or three into as many dishes as possible. It's a lot tastier and a lot easier than you might imagine.

I called this book *First We Surf, Then We Eat* because after a few hours in the water, surfers are always ready to eat well. Nothing follows the stoke of a good surf session like a good meal.

Both the food and the waves we love to devour are a transfer of energy into our bodies and souls. All energy in the physical universe moves in waves. Light waves, sound waves, radio waves, heat waves, ocean waves—waves of joy, waves of power, waves of pleasure. And there is only one place where humans actually experience this transfer of wave energy: while riding an ocean swell as it sweeps onto the shore. Surfing is a sensation of supreme pleasure that is impervious to explanation. It is physics at a level indecipherable to the uninitiated. Surfers call it "stoke."

My goal here is to inspire some of that stoke at your breakfast table, your après-surf brunch, your dinner party, your beach potluck. Eat, surf, and be merry.

Indo boat trips can open your eyes—and your tastebuds.
At Grajagan, a watery Indonesian paradise.

When people tell you they love "real"
Indonesian food, show them this photo.

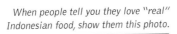

GUAM, TAHITI & THE PACIFIC
A Thousand Miles from Nowhere

I was born on the island of Guam in the northern Pacific Ocean. The nearby Mariana Trench forms a deep crescent-shaped scar on the earth's crust that cuts more than five miles below the surface of the sea. It is the world's deepest underwater valley. The nearest landmass is 1,500 miles in any direction.

The Chamorro people, who sailed here using only stars and intuition, had settled 2,000 years before Magellan, who—amazed by the speed of the native sailing vessels—named Guam the "Island of Sails." On this tiny dot where the native Taotaomona spirits still stalk the massive latte-stone pillars of ancient Chamorro holy places, I learned to surf, and I got my first tastes of vibrant cultures that were different from my own.

When a typhoon destroyed our home, we learned how to use the tropical resources of the locals instead of the military commissary's imported foodstuffs. It was a revelation. I learned, for instance, that coconuts were used to make baskets from the husks, bowls from the shells, food from the meat, and drinks from the juice. Coconut water is so much like our blood that it has been used as an emergency substitute for blood transfusions. And doesn't every perfect tropical point break have coconut palms?

From the northern Marianas to the southern Society Islands, waves and food are abundant. Anyone who loves fish, fruit, and warm-water waves can't go wrong in this part of the world.

Have gun, will travel: my formative years on Guam

Some years later, I'm surfing Huahine in Tahiti

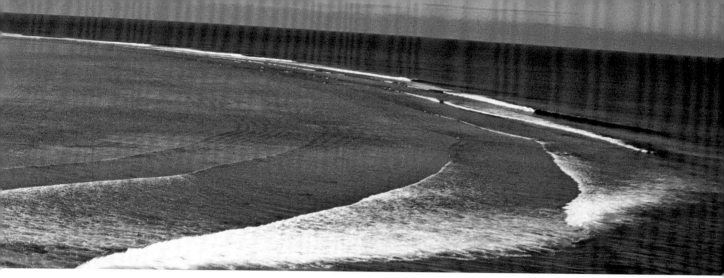

Tavarua, Fiji

Pancit Pohnepei
Noodles with Vegetables 17

Chamorro Beef Tinaktak with Finadene 19

Pisupo 21
Kalua Pork with Vegetables

Tavarua Surf Camp Banana Bread 23

Chevrettes à la Vanille et Coco 27
Tahitian Vanilla Shrimp

Palauan Papaya Upside-Down Cake 28

Stuffed Yams with Cheese, Crab & Tomatoes 31

Sashimi Française 33

Opakapaka Laulau 34
Pink Snapper in Ti Leaves with Spinach & Orange Ginger Sauce

OCEANA
Between Cancer & Capricorn

In the steaming hothouse between the Tropic of Cancer and the Tropic of Capricorn, my father had small groves of bananas, papayas, and betel nut, and he grew a half acre of corn, tomatoes, and eggplant. Under the branches of a giant Spanish flame tree, honeybees buzzed in their hive in synergy with the crackle of breakers that sounded like distant gunfire on the coral reef.

When the monsoon season drenched the patchy red soil and lured distant, sullen swells, my mother would plan our trips to "faraway places with strange-sounding names," to the patter of rain on the tin roof. She gave me my wanderlust; my father gave me my love of food. Surfing's a passion I learned on my own; it was as foreign to my parents as hieroglyphics.

During those first fourteen years that my parents lived and worked on various military bases, we traveled to nearly every corner of the Pacific: French Polynesia, Indonesia, the Carolines, Australia, the Philippines, Melanesia, Hong Kong, New Zealand, Hawaii, Japan, Micronesia, Vietnam, Taiwan, and Malaysia. They were all different. But they all had two things in common: bugs and *noodles*.

Pancit Pohnepei

Noodles with Vegetables

Pancit is the Filipino word for noodles. Marco Polo brought noodles to Europe from China, and intrepid voyagers from the Philippines brought the same noodles to the Pacific.

Note: Pancit Canton noodles are available in the Asian section of most well-stocked grocery stores.

SERVES 6

1 boneless, skinless chicken breast, diced
½ cup teriyaki sauce
2 packages Pancit Canton rice noodles
  (about 1 pound total)
4 cups warm water
2 tablespoons peanut oil, divided
1 large onion, halved and cut into ¼-inch-thick
  slices (about 1 cup)
5 cloves garlic, minced
3 green onions, diced, white and green parts
  separated

1 large red bell pepper, seeded and diced
½ small cabbage, shredded (about 2 cups)
2 celery stalks, sliced diagonally ¼ inch thick
2 carrots, sliced diagonally ¼ inch thick
  (about 1 cup)
1 tablespoon sesame oil
⅓ cup chicken broth
¼ teaspoon Chinese five-spice powder
1½ tablespoons soy sauce (more or less to taste)
Fresh lemon slices (for garnish)
¼ cup chopped fresh cilantro (for garnish)

Marinate chicken in teriyaki sauce for 20 minutes. Break noodles into 3-inch lengths and soak in warm water until they soften, about 20 minutes. Drain noodles in colander and set aside.

Heat 1 tablespoon peanut oil over high heat in a wok or 12-inch skillet. Drain chicken and discard teriyaki marinade. Stir-fry chicken for about 2 minutes, then remove and set aside.

Add second tablespoon peanut oil to wok or skillet over high heat. Add onion and stir-fry for about 2 minutes. Once onions are golden, add garlic and cook for another minute or so.

Add white parts of green onions, bell pepper, cabbage, celery, and carrots, stir-frying until just cooked through, about 3 minutes. Return chicken to wok, and continue to stir. Drop in softened noodles, and slowly add sesame oil and chicken broth. Sprinkle in five-spice powder and stir gently to let the noodles and vegetables absorb the broth. Season to taste with soy sauce.

Toss with wooden serving spoon to mix well. Garnish with lemon slices, green parts of the green onion, and chopped cilantro.

GUAM, MARIANAS ISLANDS
Surfing Submarines & Nuclear Typhoons

Guam was a fine place for surfing and a problematic site for typhoons. My friends and I learned to surf in the silt-laden river mouth at Talafofo Bay, on soft rollers like the ones in Waikiki. Slowly we graduated to reef passes that looked more like Ala Moana. Our favorite lineup in Merizo Bay broke over a sunken Japanese submarine, a casualty of World War II.

For twelve-year-olds on a remote island, the dog-eared pages of *Surfer* magazine were our only connection to the surfing world. We'd send off money orders to PO Box 1028, *Surfer*'s famous Dana Point address, requesting grainy eight-millimeter films of Greg Noll at Waimea Bay. We'd watch them endlessly—and dream on.

We incessantly scanned the naval weather maps that tracked the typhoons we hoped would come our way, bringing waves for days. Then one November the eye of one such monster took an unexpected right-angle turn and passed directly over our little island. It left everything in its wake—including the Quonset-hut home I'd grown up in—a mass of twisted wreckage.

No one knew the actual maximum velocity of Karen's wrath—all measuring devices were destroyed by its force—but estimates had gusts peaking at 185 miles per hour during the height of the storm. The US Navy report described the damage as "equal to an indirect hit from a nuclear bomb."

Chamorro Beef Tinaktak with Finadene

This is one of the Chamorro people's favorite dishes. My Guamanian friends often substitute ground beef for steak. They also add twice the chile peppers to the traditional Guam soy-vinegar-chile Finadene Sauce—which will make your mouth go nuclear.

Always remember the old Guamanian saying: *Red meat in moderation is not bad for you. Blue-green meat, no matter what the amount, is bad for you.*

SERVES 6

2 to 3 tablespoons extra-virgin olive oil

½ large onion, halved and cut into ¼-inch-thick strips

5 cloves garlic, minced

2 pounds ribeye steak, sliced very thin

2 cups long or green beans, cut in 2-inch lengths

2 cups halved cherry tomatoes, divided

1 cup fresh corn kernels

1 can coconut milk

2 tablespoons fresh lemon juice

Sea salt and freshly ground pepper to taste

2 tablespoons grated fresh coconut

Finadene Sauce (*recipe follows*)

Place large skillet over medium-high heat, add olive oil, and sauté onions for 2 to 3 minutes. Add garlic and continue to sauté for 1 minute more.

Add sliced beef and cook until browned. Drain excess liquid from skillet and add in green beans, 1 cup tomatoes, and corn. Cook until tender, about 10 minutes.

Once vegetables and beef are tender and fragrant, add coconut milk and simmer over low heat for 5 minutes. Add second cup tomatoes and lemon juice, stirring to combine. Season to taste with salt and pepper, and sprinkle grated coconut on top before serving. Serve with Finadene Sauce.

FINADENE SAUCE

1 cup soy sauce

Juice of 1 lemon

½ medium onion, thinly sliced

2 or 3 small hot chile peppers, to taste, seeded and diced

Handful of cherry tomatoes, cut in half

Combine soy sauce, lemon juice, onion, chile peppers, and tomatoes in a bowl and stir gently to combine. Store in refrigerator up to 1 week.

TUAMOTUS, FRENCH POLYNESIA
Freight on Board

The Tahitian ferryboat departed at dusk. Within minutes of leaving the harbor, open-ocean swells lunged across the bow of the vessel, throwing spray over the deck.

Maori seamen in the fifth century sailed thousands of miles through these waters in raft-like vessels. While Europe languished in the Dark Ages, these people advanced slowly down the Malay Peninsula into the Indonesian Archipelago across to the Australian continent. From New Zealand they sailed small wooden crafts, without modern navigational instruments, into the vast, unknown Pacific.

In 1981, when I first visited Polynesia's outer islands, like Huahine and the Tuamotu atolls, the freighter voyage was one of my favorite experiences. Local people used these cargo-vessel routes as a water-bound highway. To visit relatives, they booked passage on the freighters that carry goods to the various islands. Depart in the late afternoon, cross the channel, and arrive the following day, like an overnight train on a five-city run.

The Tahitians boarded in groups, bringing caged chickens, with their belongings wrapped in pareos tied to sticks. They laid their woven mats down, undid their bundles, and spread out feasts of fruit and pork and fish. And then they partied. Everyone joined in, playing ukuleles and singing and dancing hula. Even the sky participated, the stars lighting up like a million campfires overhead. And the next morning, we all woke up entering a beautiful pass to a distant island.

Checking out the waves at a Tahitian outer isle lineup

Pisupo
Kalua Pork with Vegetables

SERVES 6

1 cup chopped red cabbage
1 cup chopped green cabbage
1 cup sliced carrots, ¼ inch thick
1 cup sliced yellow summer squash,
  ¼ inch thick
1 tablespoon vegetable oil

2 cups quartered Maui sweet onions
4 pounds kalua pork *(see page 143, Rell Sunn's
  Kalua Turkey, but substitute boneless pork
  butt roast)*
Seasonings: freshly ground pepper, minced garlic,
  ginger, green onion, etc. to taste

Bring large pot of water to a boil. Add cabbage, carrots, and squash and blanch for 1 minute, then drain and set aside.

Heat vegetable oil in skillet or wok over medium-high heat. Add onions and stir-fry until just softened, about 2 minutes. Add kalua pork and cook for another minute before adding blanched vegetables and your favorite seasonings. Cook on high until meat is cooked through and vegetables are crispy and tender but not limp, about 2 minutes more. Remove from heat and serve directly from skillet or wok, or ladle onto individual plates. Serve with rice.

TAVARUA ISLAND, FIJI
"I'm the Guy"

The heart-shaped island of Tavarua is home to one of the world's most legendary surf resorts and an open-ocean reef pass considered to be the best left in the South Pacific. The late great Fijian chief Druku told me that generations ago, the native peoples named this long and powerful wave Nakuru Kuru Malagi: Thundercloud Reef.

In the early years after the discovery of the Cloudbreak reef pass off Namotu, inexperience created a false sense of safety. None of us realized how isolated the spot was, and few knew the danger of an abruptly convulsing tropical gale swirling out of the Coral Sea. The mountain ridges of Viti Levu, the largest of Fiji's 322 islands, loom across the strait. Most of the time the conditions are as pacific as this vast ocean's name—squalls are rare and usually occur at night.

South African pro and Gotcha surfwear cofounder Michael Tomson loves to recount this story about the early days of surfing there:

Michael was out on a day when the surf was good enough to keep even the most jaded rider in the lineup for hours. Although not noticeable to those focused on one of the best sessions of their lives, Dave, the boat driver and an original partner at Tavarua Surf Camp, saw the signs of an approaching squall and waved to the guys in the lineup.

The sky darkened. A wind was picking up, but the surfers were focused on the perfect sets rifling down the reef. Dave began hollering at the surfers, but they couldn't hear what he was saying because of the distance and the cracking waves. Finally, his frantic gestures sent a few guys over to the boat. When he pointed to the oncoming clouds, they scrambled aboard. A shrill rain was hissing now. The jagged mountain peaks disappeared from view, and whitecaps slapped the stern. Dave was swearing, and the guys in the boat waved and shouted at the stragglers.

Getting desperate, Dave blew the emergency horn, which finally brought in the last riders. By the time everyone got on board, the chop was as big as the length of the boat. Only Dave's expert maneuvering prevented them from capsizing. Ropes of silver rain javelined into the sea chop, plowing the surface like volleys of gunfire, stinging their eyes. Everyone was a little freaked out because Tavarua itself had disappeared from sight. Dave was driving blind.

One of the surfers spied the radio equipment under the bow as Dave pulled out the crusty life jackets and shouted, "If we get swamped, can you call the Coast Guard?"

Dave glared at him, looking like a madman. "I *AM* the Coast Guard!" he bellowed. "I'm the guy! I'm the *f*#king guy*!"

Tavarua Surf Camp Banana Bread

Tavarua Resort's kitchen staff knows the tastes of Australian, South African, American, French, and Latin surfers. The food is excellent and varied enough to suit an array of tastes. One dessert that satisfies everyone is this delicious banana bread. On a two-week stay once, I saw world title contender Jordy Smith eat an entire loaf of this stuff—and then get in line for dinner.

MAKES 2 LOAVES

3½ cups flour
3 teaspoons baking powder
1 teaspoon salt
1 teaspoon baking soda
2 cups mashed ripe banana (2 to 4 bananas)

2 tablespoons fresh lemon juice
¾ cup (1½ sticks) unsalted butter, softened
1½ cups sugar
3 eggs
¾ cup milk

Preheat oven to 350°F. Lightly grease two standard-size loaf pans. Sift together flour, baking powder, salt, and baking soda in a bowl. Set aside.

Mix mashed bananas with lemon juice. Be sure the bananas are well mashed and smooth.

In a large bowl, cream together butter and sugar until the mixture is fluffy, 2 to 3 minutes. Add eggs and beat thoroughly. Add dry ingredients to batter in small amounts, adding a little milk each time. Beat well after each addition. Fold in mashed banana and lemon juice mixture. Mix well.

Pour mixture into prepared loaf pans. Bake for about 1 hour, or until a toothpick inserted in center comes out clean. Cool and serve.

A rolling stone gathers no moss: a "bank" of stone money on Yap

*Jon Roseman, a founder of Tavarua Surf Camp,
surfs Restaurants in Tavarua.*

MOOREA, TAHITI

Did Tahitians Surf Before Hawaiians?

The Society Islands tend to slow the pace of life. Flat surf days in Tahiti are spent in leisurely pursuits: snorkeling among the schools of brightly tinted fish, strolling through gardens where Gauguin lived and painted, and sampling the Tahitian-style sashimi—raw fish marinated in lime juice and served chilled in coconut milk.

Sunsets begin the evening's entertainment, pinks and purples sliding into darkness. For me, evenings included reading the great masters of the South Seas: Robert Louis Stevenson, Herman Melville, James Michener.

Nordhoff and Hall's original *Mutiny on the Bounty* captivated me the most. While reading it, I found a passage of great intrigue: "The Indians of Tahiti rarely bathe in the sea except when a great surf is running. At such times the more daring among the men and women delight in a sport they call *horue*—swimming out among the great breakers with a light board about a fathom long, and choosing their moment to come speeding in, a quarter of a mile or more, on the crest of a high feathering sea."

Since at least one migration of Hawaii's early settlers voyaged from Tahiti, more than a thousand years ago, the *Bounty* reference would indicate that the origins of surfing might go back further than Hawaii.

Chevrettes à la Vanille et Coco
Tahitian Vanilla Shrimp

Many consider Tahitian vanilla to be the finest in the world. Tahitian shrimp is also regarded as the best. Tahitian chefs are famed for their fabulous creamy coconut and vanilla sauces. This recipe combines all of the above. If this doesn't blow your taste buds up, check your pulse—you may already be dead, but you're not in heaven.

SERVES 6

30 colossal shrimp, peeled and deveined,
   tails on (about 2 pounds)
3 tablespoons coconut oil, melted
3 tablespoons garlic, diced
2 medium white onions, 1 diced and 1 minced
¼ cup Tahitian vanilla bean extract
1 cup salted butter, cubed

½ cup Tahitian vanilla bean rum
   (use regular rum if unavailable)
¼ cup minced garlic
1 cup heavy cream
½ cup coconut milk
Sea salt and freshly ground pepper,
   to taste

Combine shrimp, coconut oil, diced garlic, diced onion, and vanilla extract in a bowl and marinate in refrigerator for 2 hours.

Heat butter in a sauté pan or skillet over medium-high heat. Add minced onion and cook for 3 minutes. Add marinated shrimp and sauté until cooked through and lightly browned, 3 to 4 minutes. Add rum and minced garlic and cook for 1 minute more. Transfer shrimp to a plate.

Pour cream and coconut milk into skillet. Reduce heat to low and simmer slowly until sauce is thickened, about 20 minutes.

When sauce is ready, return shrimp to pan. Simmer until heated through, just a few minutes. Season to taste with salt and pepper. Serve hot as an appetizer or over rice as a main course.

Palauan Papaya Upside-Down Cake

My Palauan friends (from the same Federated Micronesian island group as Yap) love making their own distilled fermented juice spirits, fishing and diving with manta rays in one of the world's most amazing lagoons, and indulging their serious penchant for sweets. This version of the upside-down cake uses papaya instead of pineapple. It's a richer, creamier version of a great dish.

SERVES 6

2 tablespoons lemon juice
2 cups sliced papaya
1 tablespoon unsalted butter
⅓ cup brown sugar
1¼ cups flour
2 teaspoons baking powder

¼ teaspoon sea salt
¼ cup shortening
¾ cup sugar
1 egg, beaten
½ cup whole milk

Preheat oven to 350°F.

Pour lemon juice over papaya and let stand 15 minutes.

Meanwhile, melt butter and brown sugar in an 8 x 8-inch glass baking dish over low heat on stovetop or in microwave. Layer papaya slices on top of sugar mixture and set aside.

In a medium bowl, sift together flour, baking powder, and salt. Set aside.

Using an electric mixer, cream shortening, then add sugar and mix well. When fully combined, add beaten egg to mixture and mix until fully incorporated. Add in sifted dry ingredients in small amounts, alternating with whole milk. Stir until fully combined.

Pour batter over sliced papaya and bake for 50 to 60 minutes, until golden brown and a toothpick inserted in the center comes out clean or with only a few crumbs attached. When cake is done, carefully turn upside down on large plate. Serve hot.

YAP, CAROLINA ISLANDS
A Continent of Mountaintops

The Pacific Ocean covers more than a third of the earth's surface. Mountains rise from its floor to form a watery continent of islands—specks of green lint on a blue blanket of open sea. On Yap, natives once sailed their bamboo canoes 280 miles west to the island of Palau, where they discovered limestone, beginning a centuries-long form of currency by carving and transporting giant disks that weigh more than a car. Millennia old, this stone currency is used to this day for such major transactions as home sales and marriage dowries.

The Yap airstrip—a black asphalt ribbon carved straight out of the jungle—was the site of a major air battle in World War II. I remember landing there at age nine and seeing a Japanese Zero on the side of the runway, a rusting hulk in the dense undergrowth. The Yapese men unloading our luggage were dressed in G-strings, carrying our bags on bamboo poles. I told my father they looked strange. His reply: "Imagine how we look to *them*. They're removing Samsonite from the belly of a great silver bird that falls out of the sky."

Such was my introduction to the continent of mountaintops.

South Pacific living

PAPEETE, TAHITI
Real Luau Style

Earlier that day, we'd watched the boats unload their catch and transport it to the marketplace. There, amid the bright floral prints of the pareos, barrels of seafood were stacked next to pyramids of papaya, striped watermelons, and golden mangoes. They say the market is not only the stomach of the islanders' life—it's the heart, too.

Arriving at dawn in the brightly colored public buses called *le truck*, the locals stream in, crowded together with their wares, music blaring out of the back. Outside the two-story steel-girded Marché Municipal, *les roulettes* (colorfully lit food trucks) serve the best inexpensive snacks in Papeete. Inside, among the fishmongers and flower stands, locals gather around the bandstand and begin to play. A ukulele, an acoustic guitar, a bass, and a pedal-steel guitar mix rhythms to play Polynesian-cowboy songs invented in the last century by native ranch hands. The lap-steel guitar technique, so integral to the Nashville sound, was actually brought from the South Pacific where it had been invented by Polynesians using instruments from Portuguese cowboys from the Madeira islands off the Atlantic coast.

In the center of the market a barbecue begins. The sounds float up lavishly through the second floor toward the tarp-like roof, mingling with aromas of the grill. The traditional Polynesian main dish is a huge wooden bowl filled with strips of suckling pig wrapped in baked taro leaves (which look and taste like spinach), sweet potatoes, and cooked baby bananas. Fill your own bowl with fresh coconut milk, dip your food in it, and eat with your fingers. The meal lasts all afternoon. As the hypnotic music plays, it's easy to pass several hours eating intermittently, sipping your Hinano and humming to the ukuleles.

Stuffed Yams with

Everything new under the shade at the Papeete market

Cheese, Crab & Tomatoes

Some say you are what you eat. Others say I yam what I yam.
— Dubious ancient proverb

SERVES 6

3 small yams (about 4 inches long by 2
  inches thick)
6 cups cooked crabmeat, flaked
2 cups roasted tomatoes, diced

4 cups (1 quart) whole milk
6 tablespoons coconut cream
Sea salt and freshly ground pepper, to taste
3 cups grated mozzarella cheese

Preheat oven to 425°F. Bake yams in their skins until soft, 40 to 50 minutes. Cut each in half lengthwise while still hot and scoop out the orange flesh into a bowl, leaving 6 skins whole in a boat shape.

Mash yam flesh with a fork. Mix in flaked crab, diced tomatoes, and milk and stir until fully combined.

Spoon 1 tablespoon coconut cream into each yam "boat." Divide yam mixture evenly among skins and season with salt and pepper to taste. Sprinkle grated cheese on top and bake until cheese is melted and bubbling, about 15 minutes.

Serve immediately.

HUAHINE, FRENCH POLYNESIA

Sashimi Anglais

In the early years at Huahine, we stayed in a small hotel owned by two French sisters in the village of Fare that looked out over the harbor where the sailboats moored and the cargo boats came and went. We often surfed Fitii, the smaller pass south of the harbor, an intense right-hander breaking far from shore. We paddled two-man outriggers, surfboards tied behind, across the lagoon where the water was pale blue and green. The reef outside was shallow; we used the coral heads to anchor our canoes, and we walked along the exposed reef wearing rubber flip-flops. When we got to the pass, we stuck reed sticks into the reef and hung our sandals on them so they wouldn't wash away. Hopping off the reef ledge into warm water, we could see the coral coming up in long, rough horns, and sometimes ducking under, our feet bumped the tips.

Fitii is quick, hollow, powerful; you have to pull in the barrel or at least get past the reef to the channel. After a couple of days of great smaller waves, I took off too late and got pitched straight down, feet first. The coral sliced my leg the way a paring knife skins an apple. Ribbons of flesh that looked just like tagliatelle, a quarter of an inch wide and fourteen inches long, hung from my thigh.

I couldn't just yank them off; scissors were needed to cut them clean. They were only one skin-layer deep, but they were oozing, and we'd been warned about sharks. They weren't normally aggressive, but now blood was in the water. I got out quickly, up on the reef, and looked around. No one noticed; the pros and the photographer were there for a cover shot.

Then Rell Sunn paddled over and asked, "Do you want to paddle in?" When I didn't answer, she said, "I'll paddle in with you."

We tied our boards to the back of an outrigger. Rell was a canoe paddler; I wasn't. Sitting behind her, I saw the muscles in her back, stroking hard. We were several hundred yards offshore with the tide rushing out, a long paddle. *I'm so glad she's here*, I thought.

Rell took me to the village first-aid clinic. One of the French sisters—proprietors of our little *pension*—snipped the slimy ribbons off, applied some salve, and smiled at me. "Lots of surfers come here for first aid," she said. "It happens to everyone sooner or later—slices just like yours." Then she smiled again and said, "We call it *sashimi anglais*."

Sashimi Française
(French Polynesian-style)

SERVES 6

1½ pounds sushi-grade yellowtail tuna,
   sliced ¼ inch thick

¼ cup lime juice, fresh if possible

¼ cup orange juice, fresh if possible

¼ cup coconut milk

1 cucumber, diced into ½-inch pieces

1 large tomato, diced into ½-inch pieces

½ teaspoon sea salt (preferably Tahitian vanilla
   fleur de sel)

2 pinches Tellicherry black pepper

2 green onions, green parts only, sliced thin

1 pinch brown sugar

Mix tuna, lime juice, orange juice, coconut milk, cucumber, tomato, sea salt, and pepper in a glass bowl. Set aside to marinate for at least 20 minutes, or up to 2 hours. Sprinkle with green onions and brown sugar and dig in.

GUAM, MARIANAS ISLANDS
A Yellowtail Tale

My father was a fisherman, and a good one. Part of the generation that could fix anything, grow anything, and make anything, he built our home beneath a windbreak of ironwood pines, high on the cliff overlooking Guam's capital city and the great Tumon Bay. From this lofty vantage point his binoculars could pick out flocks of birds feeding on schools of fish miles from shore. Since he could chart a course straight to the fish, he always came back with a catch. The local fishermen used to refer to him jokingly as "mago"—the magician. He never shared his secret with them, but he always shared his catch.

Once he spent six hours reeling in a giant ninety-eight-pound yellowtail, alone in the fourteen-foot Chris-Craft he had built himself. Just him, a rod and reel, one massive kingfish, and a long afternoon prizefight. Fifteen years after we'd left the Pacific, he still held the record for the world's largest yellowtail. In 2009—more than half a century later—the world record was still only 104 pounds.

Connor Coffin and a big, beautiful mahi mahi

Opakapaka Laulau
Pink Snapper in Ti Leaves with Spinach & Orange Ginger Sauce

Here's the best news about this dish: Unlike my dad, you don't have to sit in a little skiff, fight a huge fish for six hours, reel it in, gaff it, put it on ice, scale it, gut it, bone it, and fillet it. You just need to find a good seafood market.

Note: Ti leaves are commonly found at florist's shops, but if you can't find them, you can substitute banana leaves. And feel free to substitute another kind of snapper if you can't find opakapaka.

SERVES 6

1½ pounds opakapaka or other snapper (about 6 fillets), cut into 4-ounce pieces

2 tablespoons soy sauce
2 tablespoons peanut oil

FILLING

¼ cup peanut oil
1 cup Maui onions, thinly sliced
1 cup minced garlic
1 teaspoon chile sauce

Sea salt (Hawaiian alaea, if possible) and white pepper to taste
3 cups enoki mushrooms, stems removed
½ cup cilantro, finely chopped
8 ti leaves (or banana leaves)

ORANGE GINGER SAUCE

¼ cup water
½ cup (1 stick) unsalted butter, melted
1 teaspoon finely chopped ginger
½ teaspoon red pepper flakes
½ cup orange juice, pulp included
3 tablespoons orange marmalade

1 pound fresh baby spinach
2 blood oranges, peeled and segments divided into 6 sections
½ cup thinly sliced green onions, green parts only

Preheat oven to 350°F. In a gallon plastic bag, combine opakapaka with soy sauce and peanut oil and toss very well. Don't add any salt. Allow to marinate for at least ½ hour or up to 3 hours.

In large skillet, heat peanut oil over medium-high heat. Add onions and cook until golden, about 3 minutes. Add garlic, chile sauce, and salt and pepper; stir-fry for about 3 minutes.

Add enoki mushrooms and cilantro and cook 1 minute more. Set aside. Take two ti leaves and make a cross; cut one stem off. Take a spoonful of filling and place it in center of ti leaves. Add a piece of fish on top of filling and close ti leaves, securing packet with cooking twine. Bake opakapaka packets in glass dish covered with foil for 10 to 12 minutes.

Meanwhile, make orange ginger sauce. Add water to a small saucepan and bring to a boil. Gradually add butter, then ginger, pepper flakes, and orange juice. Cook until volume is reduced by one-fourth, then add marmalade and stir to combine. Remove from heat.

Arrange a bed of spinach on individual plates. Cut twine and remove fish from packets. Place piece of fish on spinach, and top with orange segments. Drizzle a tablespoon of orange ginger sauce over fish, sprinkle with green onions, and serve hot.

THE BASQUE COUNTRY
A Culinary Journey to the Heart of Good Living & Great Surf

LES ALCYONS, GUÉTHARY

My Salad Days in the Pays Basque

For ten years, every September found me in the Pays Basque, along the Atlantic seaboard in southwest France. Named after the Basque people who have lived there for millennia, it's a beautiful region. A glorious history. The best wines. Sweeping landscapes. Lovely women. Fabulous food. And great waves.

In those years, most of my friends were making an annual pilgrimage to Oahu's North Shore, bent on challenging the epic Hawaiian swells. Meanwhile, I was sneaking off to the Pays Basque to get uncrowded waves to myself. At first I camped in my Volkswagen van. I surfed the coast, practiced my French with the smiling, bikini-clad beach girls, and worked on my cooking skills.

Once I got the place wired, it became a tradition. Sometimes I stayed a whole year. Other times I returned home to California at Christmas and did the Hawaii wave sojourn, wintering in the warmth of the Islands. But the siren call of wine, women, and waves drew me back to France like strong minus tides. For more than a decade I never missed an autumn in the Basque country.

Mundaka river mouth

Salade Aquitaine 41

Zurrukatuna 43
Mushrooms & Shrimp

Cherries & Cheese with Black Cherry Confit 45

Basque Omelet 47

Crab Bisque 48

Madame's Moules Marinière 51
Mussels in Garlic Butter

Poulet Basquaise 52

Tuna Steaks with Onion Marmalade 54

Cousinat 57
Vegetable Casserole

Pamplona Picon Punch 59

Pintxos 60

Gâteau Basque 62

Left: Deep in the Pyrenees, where great produce comes from

SANTA MARINA, SANTANDER
The Lay of the Land

The Basque country straddles the border of
the two largest nations in Europe. To the south
and east is Castilian Spain: Hemingway's bulls
of Pamplona and the trout streams of Navarre.
To the north is the Bordeaux region of France:
fertile farmland and vineyards dotted with
châteaux. The Pyrenees provide the backdrop.
Narrow, meandering roads weave through tiny
red-tile-roofed villages, winding inland past
fertile valleys, verdant pastures, and lazy rivers.
Rugged cliffs, sheltered harbors, miles of sand
dunes, and small rocky headlands form a wave-
strewn coastline. At the border of France and
Spain, the coast snaps a right angle, a deep,
V-shaped undersea valley, a formation that acts
as a natural wedge, funneling into the Bay of
Biscay and pushing the surge into larger peaks.
Large North Atlantic swells pound the coastline
with a fierce beauty that has captivated visitors
since the Renaissance. That's why such global
surf brands as Quiksilver, Billabong, Rip Curl,
and O'Neill have their European headquarters
in the Pays Basque. A thriving surf culture helps
define the region around Biarritz.

   The Basques are renowned for their
architecture, shipbuilding, and the great game of
jai alai. But their cuisine is their most exquisite
contribution to the world. Cheeses, tapas, jambon
de Bayonne, lamb, brandies, cider, gâteau basque,
and cherries are among their many treasures.
The recipes in this chapter pay homage to this
exceptional culinary culture.

*The harbor in St-Jean-de-Luz
houses some of the best
restaurants on the Basque coast.*

Salade Aquitaine

Parts of the Basque country were appropriated by the Aquitaine kingdom back in the fifteenth century. Although they were never conquered, the Basques assimilated good recipes from their northern neighbors. Here's one of the best.

SERVES 6

1 large head Bibb or butter lettuce, torn into bite-size pieces
1 cup shredded radicchio
1 cup shredded cabbage
½ cup crumbled blue cheese
⅓ cup candied pecans
¼ cup crumbled crisp bacon

¼ cup carrots, cut into 1-inch matchsticks
1 large Anjou pear
2 ripe, firm heirloom tomatoes, diced (regular tomatoes can be substituted, but heirlooms are best)
Cracked fresh pepper, to taste

DRESSING

¼ cup fresh lemon juice
¼ cup fruity extra-virgin olive oil
2 cloves lightly roasted garlic, slivered

Pinch of crumbled fresh rosemary
¼ cup blue cheese dressing

Mix both types of lettuce, cabbage, blue cheese, pecans, bacon, and carrots in a large glass or wooden salad bowl.

To make the dressing, combine lemon juice, olive oil, garlic, and rosemary. Add in blue cheese dressing and mix well. Drizzle dressing over salad mixture and combine.

Core and slice the pear into 8 slices, leaving skin intact, and add to salad mixture.

To serve, place on individual plates or serve from salad bowl. Top with heirloom tomatoes for color, and crack fresh pepper over the salad, if you like pepper.

A Crossroads for Characters

During my early years in the Pays Basque, I crossed paths with surfers from around the globe. I brought trunks of Hawaiian shirts to sell to the local surfers and surf shops. California big-wave aficionado Keith Noel brought the first surf movies to show at the little cinema next to the old Catholic church. Surf journalist John Witzig from Sydney shared rare wines while filling his journals with all things European, later going home to start *Tracks* magazine. South African Mark Chadwick regaled us with tales from Jeffreys Bay and Tibet. British surf champ Roger Mansfield, future surf journalist Paul Holmes, and a hardy crew of English and Irish diehards joined us. Director Greg McGillivray passed through with a passel of international surf stars, filming a segment for his celebrated movie *Five Summer Stories*. And then there was Miki Dora, "Da Cat"—a surfing superstar, iconoclast, and California rogue-on-the-run. It was quite an international gallery of scamps, knaves, and rascals.

By September the tourists would be gone, and by Christmas most of the traveling surfers had headed home. That left us, a core contingent of surf expatriates and French locals. Drawn back year after year, we became a tight little clan, reveling in what seemed to be a secret world all our own. We expats and our French friends spent many evenings lingering over dinners that became increasingly more elaborate. That was the beginning of my love affair with food, surf travel—and writing.

Discovering Basque bakery bliss at the Old Mill; see pages 62–63 for more

Zurrukatuna
Mushrooms & Shrimp

This recipe combines the earthy flavor of mountain mushrooms with the briny brightness of fresh shellfish—a healthy marriage of surf and turf.

SERVES 6

2 tablespoons salted butter

1 pound medium shrimp, peeled and deveined

1 large portobello mushroom, chopped

6 to 10 cremini mushrooms (or 10 to 12 button mushrooms), thinly sliced

1 leek, rinsed and finely chopped

1 tablespoon finely chopped fresh oregano

¼ teaspoon freshly ground black pepper

Hearty pinch of bacon bits (optional)

⅓ cup red table wine, preferably French

Heat large skillet over medium-high heat. Add butter and shrimp and sauté lightly for 1 minute on each side.

Add both kinds of mushrooms, cover, and cook for 5 minutes. Do not stir—this allows the mixture to glaze. Uncover and stir in chopped leek, oregano, pepper, and bacon bits (if using). Stir in wine. Cover and simmer for another 5 minutes, stirring occasionally to prevent burning.

Place shrimp and mushroom mixture on serving plate or serve right from pan. Either way, scrape pan bottom to release glaze. It's good stuff.

PLAYA DE GROS, SAN SEBASTIÁN

Last Supper at the General's Table

Miki Dora was the Black Knight of surfdom. The monarch of Malibu surfed with astonishing beauty and arrogant aplomb. Shoving other riders off his waves and making iconoclastic pronouncements to a slavering media, "Da Cat" was superbly stylish, with brooding Brando looks and an effortless athleticism. He epitomized the *Easy Rider* anti-hero style of the turbulent 1960s. His penchant for easy living—and his willingness to play fast and loose with a system he considered corrupt—pushed his behavior to the legal limits...and beyond. Like George Clooney's loner in *Ocean's Eleven,* Miki lived fast and evaded a long string of criminal investigators bent on yanking his surf leash. On the lam, he staked out extradition-free places in France and South Africa, a relentless nomad surfing every day like it was his last. Miki and I spent the better part of a decade hanging out among the locals and vagabond surf gentry in the Basque country—he as a fugitive and me as a youth set on wasting my career chances.

Miki hated losing. He could best the best of us at tennis, golf, backgammon, handball, and, of course, surfing. There was, however, one game I could consistently beat him at: Ping-Pong. When our seashore village shuttered itself against big-storm winter days, we'd thread our way between penetrating downpours to the community center and smack that little hollow ball for hours. Feeling overconfident one day, I bet him a dinner in San Sebastián, just across the border in Spain. I learned a lesson the hard way: never bet Miki. When there was a bet on the line, he'd elicit some paranormal performance from within. Which is exactly what he did.

Naturally he picked the finest restaurant in San Sebastián and asked for the best table in the house. The proprietor gave us "the General's table." Set on an elevated patio in the town square, it was normally reserved for the top regional commander in charge of hunting down Basque insurgents. At the time, Basque separatists stood at the height of their struggle for independence, and their revulsion for Spanish dictator Franco's military repression had led to open warfare. Bombs were going off every week somewhere—but we were blissfully unfazed.

Lunch was memorable—crab bisque, tapas, a seafood platter, cherries with cheese, and fine wine. But it was more than the food that made the meal unforgettable.

Two days later, Miki brought me a newspaper. "Terrorists Kill General" the headline proclaimed. The taste of sour wine rose up in my throat. The day after our visit, separatists had gunned down the General in a drive-by shooting, at the very "General's table" where we'd just dined. It kept us from going back for quite a while. A last supper for both us and that general.

Cherries & Cheese with Black Cherry Confit

This is a super-simple dessert—take some great Basque cheese, like an Ardi Gasna from Fromagerie Pardou (but any good semihard sheep's-milk cheese will work), some cherry confit (or cherry jam), and some black cherries, and you have everything you need.

Basque black cherries thrive in the cool Pyrenees mountains climate; the most famous ones come from a town called Itxassou. But your local cherries will work just fine.

Slowly heat up some cherry jam, add some fresh cherries, and cook gently until the cherries soften. Pour this confit over the cheese, open a bottle of red wine from Domaine Ilarria of Irouléguy, and the afternoon will become blissful. Just keep an eye out for Basque separatists....

Join the Club

Basque chefs were among the first to use foods from the Americas—they became masters of chocolate, they incorporated tomatoes and corn into many traditional dishes, and they made the pepper a national icon. Basque men consider cooking a fine art form. In more than a thousand gastronomic societies, men get together to cook, eat, and socialize. Called *txokos,* these elite cooking clubs are food-centered fraternities, traditionally all male.

Basque dishes are not based on elaborate sauces or vast arrays of spices. The excellence of Basque cooking is due to the use of quality local ingredients in season, combined with preparations that enhance rather than mask the natural flavors. Fresh, locally grown meats and produce are the most important components of Basque cuisine.

Basque Omelet

Made with onions, peppers, and tomatoes, pipérade is a typical sauce of the region, commonly served on the side to accompany meat or fish. Full of flavor, this omelet combines pipérade with beaten eggs to make an easy, impressive, one-pan main course in only half an hour.

SERVES 6

3 to 4 tablespoons extra-virgin olive oil
1 medium onion, thinly sliced
½ medium sweet yellow pepper, cut into
   ¼-inch dice (I use the yellow for color,
   but red is fine)
1 medium green bell pepper, cut into
   ¼-inch dice

2 ounces *jambon de Bayonne* ham, diced
   (substitute prosciutto if not available)
2 cloves garlic, finely chopped
2 ripe round tomatoes, each cut into 8 pieces
4 large eggs
½ cup light cream
Sprinkle of cheese (optional)

Heat oil in a deep 10-inch skillet over medium heat. Sauté onion, peppers, and ham until onion turns soft and golden, about 6 minutes. Add garlic and sauté for 2 more minutes.

Add tomato chunks and continue to cook until onions are almost caramelized and peppers are cooked. (Don't let vegetables stick to pan—if they do, add a little water and a tiny bit of oil and stir.)

Beat eggs and cream in small bowl and pour evenly over vegetables in pan. Let them sit without stirring. Cook over low heat until eggs set. Add a sprinkle of your favorite cheese (if using). Cover pan until tops of eggs are fully cooked. Remove from heat and serve from pan in slices.

Crab Bisque

This was the recipe that won me the finale of the soup competition (see story below). It's not hard to make, and the result will make you a hit with your buds (and their taste buds).

SERVES 6

2 tablespoons unsalted butter

1 medium onion, finely chopped

1 medium carrot, finely chopped

1 celery rib, finely chopped

4 large cloves garlic, crushed

½ teaspoon fresh thyme leaves

¼ teaspoon black pepper

½ cup cognac

1½ cups chicken broth

½ cup dry white wine

1 pound lump crabmeat, left at room
  temperature for 30 minutes

3 cups half & half

1½ cups heavy cream

3 tablespoons tomato paste

2 teaspoons fresh lemon juice

1 teaspoon tarragon, chopped into ribbons

Large pinch cayenne

Sea salt, to taste

6 tablespoons sour cream or crème fraîche

6 fresh chives, snipped to ½-inch lengths

Heat butter in large pot over medium-high heat. Add onion, carrot, celery, garlic, thyme, and pepper and sauté until vegetables are soft, about 3 minutes.

Stir in cognac, then add chicken broth, white wine, and 2 ounces of the crab. Reduce heat and simmer for about 20 minutes.

Gradually whisk in half & half, cream, and tomato paste, stirring gently, until bisque thickens, about 5 minutes. Once thickened, stir in lemon juice, tarragon, and cayenne. Taste and season with salt as needed.

To serve, transfer hot bisque to 6 shallow bowls and divide remaining crab among them, spooning some into the middle of each bowl. Drizzle with sour cream and sprinkle with chives.

LA FITENIA, GUÉTHARY
The Soup Contests

On rainy winter days when the surf was too stormy, we'd become our own little cooking club, making and sharing meals. Soups were the most popular; everybody likes soup, and it's usually cheap and easy to make.

The infamous Basque surf soup contests originated when Miki Dora, our reigning connoisseur of style and taste, challenged the chefs in the crew to a cook-off. Miki and his girlfriend, Linda, had stayed with us for several seasons, and a few expats had been bragging about our cooking skills. Miki knew he would eat for free—which was one of the prime elements of his ethos. We got immediate buy-in from the local French surfers and their girlfriends, who agreed to serve as judges and tasters, and to make sure that no shenanigans (like packaged ingredients) were used. Everything had to be made from scratch. After a series of soup contests that turned into long, festive banquets, Miki decreed that a grand feast would be held to determine the season's premiere surf chef.

After I showed a little creativity and lots of pre-contest prep, Miki declared me the winner after a unanimous vote from the French judging panel. It was a huge impetus in my lifelong passion for cooking.

CHAMBRE D'AMOUR, ANGLET
Le Sable d'Or

Le Sable d'Or sat on the waterfront below the edge of the Côte Basque cliffs, looking across the dunes that end at the Adour River in Bayonne and the long jetty at La Barre. From under its colored umbrellas, you could watch the fine waves that broke consistently almost year-round. It was an unpretentious little bistro that served morning coffee, food all day, and, after dinner, cognac and pastis. The owner, whom we knew as Madame Vacher, was a classic French proprietor who catered to visiting surfers. It was a hangout for many a lonely surf traveler, and Madame made sure we were all well fed. She always offered *un sandwich australien* and *une salade américaine,* and in the cold winter months when the crowds were gone, you could sit inside all day for the price of a beer.

This snug little eatery was the first place I ever tasted mussels, and to this day I have never seen anyone improve on this recipe. There may be fancier restaurants in Paris and more Michelin stars in Lyon, but here on the west coast of France, the stars are the many family-owned establishments that serve simple, flat-out delicious food. Every surfer who ever passed through Anglet owes Madame a debt of gratitude.

Madame's Moules Marinière
Mussels in Garlic Butter

Serve a glass of wine with this classic dish. As W.C. Fields once said, "I always cook with wine. Sometimes I even add it to the food."

SERVES 6

3 dozen mussels

2 shallots, finely chopped

6 cloves garlic, minced (you can't have too much for this recipe!)

2 sprigs fresh thyme

1 bay leaf

¾ cup dry white wine

4 tablespoons (½ stick) unsalted butter, cubed

1 bunch flat-leaf parsley, finely chopped

Rinse mussels in cold water, and scrub and scrape to remove any barnacles or dirt. Discard any with broken shells, and make sure all the mussels you use are live and closed. Let them sit in cold water for a couple of hours until ready to use.

Put shallots, garlic, thyme sprigs, bay leaf, and white wine into large, deep skillet or pot and sauté over medium-high heat to bring out the flavors, 1 to 2 minutes. Turn the heat down to a simmer and cook gently for 10 minutes. Turn heat back up to medium high, then drain mussels and slide them gently into pot. Cover and allow to steam until most have opened, about 3 minutes.

Add butter and put lid back on for 30 seconds to allow butter to melt. Add parsley and shake pan well to distribute, then serve immediately, discarding any mussels that remain closed. Serve with crusty bread to mop up the delicious, garlicky broth.

Poulet Basquaise

One late autumn day, I ate this dish for the first time at Pierre Gascogne's home. I met Pierre on my second trip to the Basque country, when we were twenty-two. He became the founding publisher of *Surf Session* in France, and I became the publisher of *Surfer*. (Must have been something in the wine.) We have remained great friends all these years, and I still cook Poulet Basquaise every chance I get. Like a lot of things the French do with food, it is a simple masterpiece in a one-pot dish. Genius.

Note: Piment d'Espelette is a Basque paprika that's available at most specialty supermarkets or online.

SERVES 6

¼ cup extra-virgin olive oil, divided
3 onions, sliced (as one would for fajitas)
3 cloves garlic, chopped
4 sweet bell peppers, sliced (same as onions—
 I use 2 green and 2 yellow for color)
2 pounds tomatoes, coarsely chopped

6 small, skinless, bone-in chicken breasts
4 skinless, bone-in chicken thighs
1 cup white wine
½ to 1 cup chicken stock
Piment d'Espelette, to taste
Sea salt and freshly ground pepper, to taste

In a deep saucepan, heat 2 tablespoons olive oil over medium-high heat. Add onions and garlic, and let them become golden, stirring, about 3 minutes. Add bell peppers and tomatoes, and cook for 10 minutes over low heat.

In another saucepan, heat remaining 2 tablespoons oil. Fry chicken pieces until golden, about 3 minutes per side. Transfer chicken to saucepan with vegetables.

Pour in white wine. Add ½ cup or more chicken stock if needed to cover chicken. Cover and let simmer for about 40 minutes, occasionally stirring and tasting regularly. When the sauce is cooked down, add piment d'Espelette, salt, and pepper to taste.

Poulet Basquaise is traditionally served over white rice, but you can substitute brown rice. Zucchini and eggplant are sometimes added to the dish by the Basques, depending on what else is being served.

GRANDE PLAGE, BIARRITZ

The Sun Also Rises on Basque Waves

In 1957, the first surfboard arrived in France with California screenwriter Peter Viertel, who was on location in Pamplona for the filming of Ernest Hemingway's *The Sun Also Rises*. Passing through Biarritz, he knew instantly that he had discovered a new wave field. Fascinated with the empty waves and the beauty of the Basque coast, Viertel immediately sent home for his surfboard. Thus began the Basque surf culture.

Low tide in the corner of the Côte de Basque, Biarritz

Tuna Steaks with Onion Marmalade

The Basques are great fishermen. They bring boatloads of tuna and cod into the little port of Saint-Jean-de-Luz, and during tuna season they grill freshly cleaned tuna steaks like this right out in the park next to the docks along the harbor. In this recipe, onions are cooked with sherry, sugar, bay leaves, and peppercorns to create a caramelized onion marmalade. It adds a great kick to fresh tuna, and you can do it on the grill just before you cook the fish.

SERVES 6

6 large yellow onions, thinly sliced
½ cup sherry or wine vinegar
3 cups sugar
20 black peppercorns, cracked

1 bay leaf
1½ pounds fresh ahi tuna, cut into 6 portions
Extra-virgin olive oil as needed
1 teaspoon piment d'Espelette

Light a charcoal grill and bring to medium-low heat or preheat a gas grill to 325°F.

To make onion marmalade, heat an iron skillet over low heat on a range (or on cooler edge of grill) and add onions, sherry or wine vinegar, sugar, peppercorns, and bay leaf. Cook on low heat until liquid has almost evaporated and onions are translucent, about 15 minutes. Transfer to bowl and set aside.

Brush tuna pieces on both sides with olive oil. Place on hot grill and cook for 2 minutes on each side, basting with a little oil and sprinkling with some piment d'Espelette. You want to just sear the ahi to retain its tenderness, texture, and flavor, like a steak.

Transfer ahi to a serving platter or plates and top with onion marmalade. It's delicious served over rice with sautéed peppers and mushrooms, but it's spectacular on a bed of green lentils cooked to a creamy consistency.

BELHARRA, SAINT-JEAN-DE-LUZ
Seafood & Monster Surf

Saint-Jean-de-Luz has been famous for seafood for centuries. In 1660, Louis XIV married his queen, Maria Theresa, at the church in Saint-Jean-de-Luz and set up his summer residence there. The royal feast that followed set the stage for fine dining in a town previously best known as a pirate haven. The twentieth century saw it become a popular beach resort—a surf spot with good surf shops—but it was mostly noted for its quaint architecture, beachfront restaurants, and outstanding fish and shellfish dishes.

Then, in the twenty-first century, it became famous for the discovery of a massive rideable wave at Belharra, just outside the harbor. Although known to local surfers for nearly a decade, it exploded into the public consciousness when photos appeared on the internet. Now it's one of the dozen global locations on the big-wave circuit when winter storms create gigantic surf. Jamie Mitchell, Surfline's 2017 Best Performance Award winner, rides big Belharra as well as anyone alive. He also knows good fish when he tastes it and is an avid spear fisherman—just not when Belharra is breaking. And like my dad, his father loves fishing too, and both taught their sons to fish. My dad just didn't get a surfing legend in the bargain.

Jamie Mitchell at Belharra in the Basque Country

MUNDAKA, BISCAY
Ocean Explorers

The Basques are one of the great seafaring and shipbuilding cultures of history. Long before Columbus set out on his voyage, the Basques were harvesting cod from the fishing banks off Newfoundland. In fact, one of the reasons Columbus was so sure he'd find land if he kept sailing west was because he took Basque pilot Juan de la Cosa on his voyage. La Cosa continued to comb the Caribbean basin, and in 1500 drew the first map of the world that included the Americas. Another Basque seafarer, Sebastián Vizcaíno, was an early explorer of the California coast, discovering Monterey, mapping Baja and San Diego Bay, and sailing north of San Francisco, in the process giving California many of its present-day names. And while Magellan is given credit for first circumnavigating the globe, it was actually his Basque pilot, Juan Sebastián de Elcano, who completed the voyage after Magellan was killed by natives in the Philippines. Basque sailors and Basque-made vessels explored the coasts of Africa and Asia, no doubt discovering countless perfect waves long before their usefulness was known.

The wave at Mundaka is one of the world's best lefts, and Juan de la Cosa, born not thirty miles from there, undoubtedly sailed past it before he left to discover the Americas.

Cousinat
Vegetable Casserole

I first tasted this dish in Ainhoa, a tiny, gorgeous village in the foothills of the Pyrenees, but it is a specialty in the Biscay town of Bayonne. We were on our way to a winter snowboard session after a good snowfall in the mountains and wanted something filling before we hit the lifts, but not something that was going to slug us out. This was perfect.

If you're trying to get your vegetables in, I highly recommend *cousinat*. It's loaded with nutrients, tastes fantastic, and goes with almost any fish or meat (especially *jambon de Bayonne*—a cured ham produced only in France) served over rice.

SERVES 6

1 tablespoon extra-virgin olive oil

2 slices jambon de Bayonne (or prosciutto), diced

12 green onions, trimmed

1 red bell pepper, seeded and thinly sliced

6 artichoke hearts

3 small carrots, peeled and thinly sliced

4 ounces green beans, trimmed

4 ripe tomatoes, coarsely chopped

1 pound broad beans, shelled and peeled

6 tablespoons dry white wine

Sea salt and freshly ground pepper, to taste

Place a deep 12-inch skillet over medium-high heat, add oil, and lightly brown diced ham. Add green onions, bell pepper, artichoke hearts, and carrots, and cook, stirring, for about 2 minutes. Mix in green beans, tomatoes, and broad beans, and cook for 10 minutes, stirring often.

Add wine and boil for 5 minutes, stirring regularly. Season to taste with salt and pepper. Reduce heat to low, cover, and simmer for 1 hour. You'll know it's done when the vegetables are tender and coated with a syrupy glaze. Serve equal portions in a bowl over rice.

PLAZA DEL TOROS, PAMPLONA
Running with the Bulls

In the second week of July, in Spain's Basque Navarre region, the San Fermín festival unfolds, an event that (depending on your perspective) is either a glorious celebration of Latin tradition or a sangria-soaked spectacle of insanely reckless bravado and bedlam.

Every year since 1591, hundreds of adrenaline-fueled celebrants, many of whom have been drinking all night, gather in a main square in Pamplona. Thousands of onlookers have already taken their places along the 900-yard route of curving, climbing streets that lead to a bullring packed with more screaming spectators.

The summer after my sophomore year in college, I traveled Europe with college chums, taking in the Cannes Film Festival, the Grand Prix in Monte Carlo, and the legendary second Glastonbury music festival. It was a heady five months, but none of it could match the running of the bulls in Pamplona. The year before, several runners had reportedly been killed; by the time we had built up the bravado to participate on day three, at least a dozen crazed Spaniards had been gored, butted, or trampled. The goal is to run in front of the stampeding herd to reach the bullring without injury. For seven days this ritual repeats, pitting each morning's crew of hapless hedonists against a posse of burly beasts that are nearly as scared as the participants—which only makes them more dangerous.

When the 8 a.m. starting gun (a rocket) goes off, the bulls are let loose and the square's sea of participants empties like a chamber of an Uzi automatic. From there it's an unnerving half-mile sprint to stay ahead of the bulls. In front is a blinding blur of red scarves and white shirts; behind is a deafening roar of hooves and screams.

I had given my camera to a girlfriend in our crew, and when we reached the underpass where I knew she'd be aiming the lens, I tried to slow down enough to get close to the bulls for a few seconds. It was a miscalculation—a bull on my left periphery surged ahead, battering a hapless runner into the wall like a rag doll. It made for a good photo at least.

At the finish, you run into a long, pitch-dark tunnel leading into the bullring. In the darkness all you can sense is the sound of gasping breaths and the smell of fear; in that moment your only prayer is to avoid tripping and piling up in a blind heap, just waiting for a collision with the frantic, snorting animals behind you. Breaking out into the blinding sunlight of the bullring amid the bellow of the bota bag-swilling crowd is a rush akin to bursting to the surface of the ocean after a two-wave hold-down. A quick vault over the head-high barricades and life has never felt so exhilarating.

Emboldened by survival, I ran twice more that year and several times again in years after.

It is nothing, of course, compared to a surf session at giant Mavericks, a steep run in avalanche country, or actual combat in the mountains of Afghanistan. So many souls have survived the San

Fermín experience in the decades since my runs that it seems almost overstated now. But for sheer spectacle, looking back at that thundering herd gaining on me as we entered the final stretch is a memory that still thrills.

Pamplona Picon Punch

This drink was created in Bakersfield by Basque shepherds and brought back to their homeland, where it has become a staple aperitif.

After our run with the bulls, we had a couple of these. Nothing calms the nerves better, especially if accompanied by pintxos of ham, olives, and cheese (see next page for more on that). If you've just run with the bulls in Pamplona, order two of these punches and send me the bill.

SERVES 6

Crushed ice
2 ounces Torani Amer liqueur
1 teaspoon grenadine
Splash club soda

Splash fresh lemon juice
1 lemon slice
1 jigger cognac or brandy

Fill glass with crushed ice. Pour in Torani Amer liqueur and top with grenadine. Fill rest of glass with club soda and a little lemon juice.

Stir gently, and rub rim of glass with lemon slice, then add it to the drink. Float the bit of brandy on top of the soda, and enjoy.

Pintxos

Pintxos are the Basque version of Spanish tapas, the small appetizers that are served everywhere in southern France and northern Spain. They're perfect for watching sports on TV with a cold beer, hanging at the beach with a good bottle of Bordeaux, or serving a lot of hungry guests before a main meal.

Pintxos generally start with a small slice of bread or toast (sliced baguettes are ideal) topped with any number of items: chunks of ham, cheese, chorizo, salami, olives, shrimp, artichoke hearts, eggplant, meatballs, mushrooms, sardines, roasted peppers, fried zucchini, and so much more, in any combination that suits you. Usually two or three items is the limit. They're held in place by a toothpick—a pintxo—the little sword that "pierces."

Pintxos don't have to be on bread with toothpicks. They can also be served in small dishes with a sauce. Scallops, chicken, calamari, pork, and mushrooms are just a few of the possibilities.

My favorite pintxo with Basque ingredients:

Jambon de Bayonne

Idiazabal semihard goat cheese

Grilled mushroom caps

Zopako (a crusty bread made by one of the best bakers in San Sebastián)

Extra-virgin olive oil

Balsamic vinegar

Pile the ham, cheese, and grilled mushrooms on a slice of bread flavored with a dip of olive oil and a splash of balsamic vinegar. The combo will start a party in your mouth that will get up and dance. If you can't get the Basque ingredients, no worries—just substitute prosciutto, Manchego cheese, and a crusty baguette from your favorite bakery.

LES CAVALIERS, CHAMBRE D'AMOUR, ANGLET

An Ancient Ancestry

The fiery Basques are Europe's oldest people. Their origins are still a mystery; most historians believe they descended from the Neolithic period and somehow stayed intact through centuries of invasions, wars, and repressions. They proudly cling to a language that is unrelated to any Indo-European tongue. They're noted for their distinctive folklore, folk theater, games, music, and a light-footed, acrobatic form of dancing. They have never been conquered, and they have maintained their cultural independence while fighting off Romans, Visigoths, Arabs, Moors, and Franco's Spain. Their culture is unlike any other in Europe or anywhere else. Even their DNA is unique. And so is their food.

MILADY, BIDART
The Old Mill

About a mile and a half inland of the little beach town of Bidart is an old mill, Le Moulin de Bassilour, which bakes the best bread, cakes, and cookies in a wood oven. A picture-postcard structure built in 1741, it still uses the centuries-old method of milling flour with large wheels powered by the stream. (See the Old Mill photo on page 40.)

Before an afternoon surf session, we'd drive out to the mill to get its famous gâteau. If the scent of baking bread filled the air before our car reached the stone bridge, the wind was offshore and the surf conditions optimum. If we couldn't detect the aroma till after we'd crossed the bridge, the wind was onshore and it was a good idea to stop and relax over a snack. Besides the gâteau, I've always loved the mill's lemon cookies. Pro surfer and brilliant blogger Coco Ho always gets them when she comes to the Roxy Pro here. Coco's favorite food is cookies, so she should know.

Gâteau Basque

Famous in the region, this pie-like cake is delicious and pretty easy to make. If you're pressed for time, feel free to substitute a ready-made pie crust and skip making the dough.

MAKES ONE 8- OR 9-INCH GÂTEAU

DOUGH

2 cups all-purpose flour

⅓ cup ground almonds or almond flour

1½ teaspoons baking powder

½ teaspoon sea salt

¾ cup (1½ sticks) unsalted butter, softened

1 cup sugar

3 egg yolks

1 teaspoon vanilla extract

CUSTARD FILLING

¾ cup milk

½ cup heavy cream

3 egg yolks

⅓ cup sugar

3 tablespoons cornstarch

1 teaspoon vanilla or almond extract

Cooked cherries, lightly mashed (optional)

To make the dough: In large bowl, combine flour, ground almonds, baking powder, and salt. Set aside. In bowl of a stand mixer, combine butter and sugar, and beat at medium speed until creamy. Add egg yolks and vanilla and mix until smooth.

Keep speed at medium and slowly add flour mixture. Beat until thoroughly combined and mixture clings together when pressed against side of bowl. Divide into two portions, with one portion slightly larger than the other. Flatten each into a disk, wrap tightly in plastic wrap, and refrigerate at least 1 hour, or up to 2 days.

Next, make the custard filling. Heat milk and cream gently in a medium saucepan over medium-low heat. Meanwhile, while that heats, whisk together egg yolks, sugar, and cornstarch in a medium bowl. When milk mixture is hot, slowly drizzle yolk mixture into saucepan while vigorously whisking. Cook over medium heat, stirring constantly, until custard becomes very thick. (If lumps form, whisk until smooth.) Stir in vanilla. Transfer custard to medium bowl. Place plastic wrap directly on top of custard. Refrigerate 30 minutes.

Preheat oven to 400°F. Butter bottom and sides of 8- or 9-inch springform pan.

Roll larger portion of dough into 10 1/2-inch round (dough will be thick). Place in bottom of pan, pressing excess dough up inside edge of pan so it hangs a little over rim.

Add cooled custard filling, spreading evenly almost to edges of circle. Roll remaining dough into 9-inch round. Place on top of filling, and press edges of dough with bottom layer to seal and form a rim. Set pan on baking sheet and bake for 20 minutes. Reduce heat to 350°F and continue baking until gâteau is golden brown, about 15 minutes longer.

Cool on a wire rack for at least 45 minutes before serving. Remove pan sides and slice using a serrated knife. Serve with cooked cherries, if you have them. Refrigerate remaining cake after serving.

CALIFORNIA
Leading the Quest for Ingenuity & Healthy Cuisine

The Left Coast's mania for healthy eating combined with surfing's explosive popularity has spawned a culture known for both wave riding and great food. It's been my home base for many years now.

As one of the world's three largest capitals of surfing (along with Hawaii and Australia), California has had a huge impact on surf culture. And its influence on American—and even global— cooking is indisputable. The fusion revolution, which started in California's coastal enclaves, has melded six continents of cuisine into a whole new realm of great eating.

I learned to cook as I traveled in my global search for good surf. But my culinary experience came of age at Margarita's Village, my own outpost in the food world. My restaurateur days are long gone (thank goodness), but I'm still at heart a California cook.

The San Clemente pier: a place to watch the surf and eat at Fisherman's

The estuary that creates the great Lower Trestles waves is full of fish.

Margarita's Village Mango Margarita 67

Fig Jam Pizza with Goat Cheese, Prosciutto & Arugula 69

Foiled Again 70
Grilled Fish & Vegetable Packet with Donald Takayama's Teriyaki Sauce

Roasted Vegetables with Caramelized Balsamic Glaze 75

Pasta Carbonara 77

Half Moon Bay Salad 79
Crab, Artichoke, Avocado & Pistachio Salad with Lime Cilantro Dressing

Quesadilla Kempton 85

Surfwise Steel-Cut Oatmeal 86

SAN CLEMENTE, CALIFORNIA
It Takes a Margarita's Village

In the waning years of my wasted youth, I bought a restaurant on the north end of San Clemente, on Pacific Coast Highway between the freeway and the beach. I went in with three Mexican partners, who had a raging hot spot in Tijuana known for fourteen flavors of margaritas. We patterned the look and feel of it after their place in Tijuana, restoring an old Spanish Colonial building and fashioning a menu of dishes from the various regions of Mexico—a novel and (as it turned out) popular idea at the time. We brought in some great line cooks, and my wife ran the service staff. Restaurants are a great business if you like working fourteen-hour days in conditions just slightly less stressful than combat. It was great fun, though, and we won an award from a respected critics' group for our food.

Restaurants are living, breathing entities imbued with personality—a small society that combines theatrics, psychology, and assembly-line surgery with an unpredictable market-research project, all in a wildly unstable customer environment. They sell ambience more than sustenance. Their economics are voodoo, their life spans unknown. They can catch a disease and collapse in a week, or live a robust, prosperous life and then suffer a protracted, painful demise. And yet almost everyone at one time or another imagines owning one. They mistake *enjoying* a restaurant for the vastly different reality of *operating* one. It's a delusion.

My wife and I used to joke about starting a support group called Restaurants Anonymous for those addicted to the idea of starting down that path to destruction. We envisioned a hotline. *Don't move—we'll be right there! Don't do anything rash.* We'd talk would-be restaurateurs off the ledge of the liquor license, the abyss of the authentic enchilada. Although our little inside joke was intended to amuse ourselves, it wasn't actually comical—or untrue. Restaurants opened by compulsive food lovers have ravaged more life savings than the Mexican drug cartels.

The Cheer of Living Dangerously

When Bruce Beach sold his surf sunglass company, Electric, he was already on his way to being one of the most successful entrepreneurs in the surf industry. Then he started the Peligroso tequila brand and made it a top-flight spirit, bringing in such legends as big-wave superstar Greg Long to keep the vibe authentic. *Peligroso* ("dangerous" in Spanish) is the way both Greg and Bruce have lived their lives—not without insight and preparation, but with a willingness to take risks and a calculated defiance of danger.

As with all brothers of the surfing tribe, I support Bruce's products; he's a friend and a core surfer with a free spirit and a good heart. But I drink his tequila because it's as good as it gets. Cheers to living dangerously!

Margarita's Village Mango Margarita

At our restaurant we concocted fourteen flavors of margaritas. This was our most popular.

MAKES 2 COCKTAILS

3 juicy limes

1 teaspoon sugar

1 cup fresh or frozen mango, cubed

½ cup crushed ice

3 ounces Peligroso silver tequila

1 ounce triple sec or other orange liqueur

3 ounces freshly squeezed orange juice

Kosher salt (optional)

Zest limes with grater. Pour sugar over lime zest and toss with your fingers to combine. Set aside, and slice zested limes.

Throw mango into a blender and top it off with some of the ice. Add tequila, triple sec, orange juice, lime zest, and remaining ice, and blend until smooth.

To serve, use a slice of lime to moisten rim of glasses, and add salt to rim, if you like it. Pour drinks and serve frosty immediately.

LOWER TRESTLES, ORANGE COUNTY
The Surf Virus

Owning a restaurant in a surf community means hiring surfers. In San Clemente, young men and women who want flexible schedules and a fun work environment comprise the predominant employee pool. Most days, the morning surf satisfied my waiters and cooks who rode waves. They were, on average, as punctual and diligent as anyone you might hire in any laid-back Southern California beach town. Most had the added benefit of being friends or kids of our patrons. That gave the restaurant a family atmosphere that added to our local vibe.

These waiters and cooks also served as surf forecasters. I always knew a great swell was on the way when the night before, the first of them would call in sick. By 10 a.m., two more would have come down with a serious virus. The smart employee would call in just before we opened and say the doctor told him it was an infectious virus and, as proof, offer to present a physician's note proving he was to stay home so the virus didn't spread. Which proved one thing: doctors surf, too.

Meanwhile, customers would flow through all day long, raving about the perfect swell now hitting Lower Trestles. Later in the evening, the invariable employee who hadn't even bothered to call would leave a message: "Sorry, I came down with a really bad virus. Been laid up all day. Finally feeling better now. Should be in tomorrow. This virus has really taken a lot of people out."
Yep. Surf viruses will do that.

Fig Jam Pizza with Goat Cheese, Prosciutto & Arugula

I know, I know, you can't imagine fig being good on pizza. But it isn't just good—it's epic. I like to use a Boboli or a thin, ready-made pizza crust, but get any premade crust you like. Making pizza crust from scratch is not realistic in many kitchens and impossible on the road, but you can if you prefer. This recipe was inspired by a dish at the Privateer in Oceanside, owned by two friends of mine, Charlie Anderson and Jamie Stone, both core surfers, surf publishing professionals, and great restaurateurs. Don't miss a visit if you're in town.

SERVES 6

1 (12-inch) pizza crust, store-bought or
  homemade

Olive oil & cooking spray as needed

3 tablespoons fig jam

2 tablespoons marinara sauce (bottled is fine)

1 small log goat cheese (about 5 ounces)

3 ounces mozzarella cheese, shredded

1 ounce (1 package) thinly sliced prosciutto,
  torn into 1-inch strips

3 cups arugula, divided

½ cup shaved parmesan cheese

Pomegranate seeds for garnish (optional)

Preheat oven or charcoal or gas grill to high heat, about 425°F.

Place crust on a round pizza pan that has been sprayed with cooking spray or oil. Lightly drizzle olive oil all over pizza crust, and spread fig jam evenly over crust.

Once fig jam layer is down, spread marinara sauce evenly over pizza crust. Be sure not to overload crust—too much sauce will make it soggy and heavy to eat once cut into pieces.

Drop small chunks of goat cheese across pizza, making sure there is some on each potential slice. Sprinkle sauced pizza with mozzarella, and drape prosciutto strips over the cheese. Finally, scatter about 1 cup arugula over toppings.

Set pizza in oven or grill, and bake until bottom of crust is crisp, about 10 minutes.

When done to your liking, remove from heat and let sit for 3 minutes. Scatter remaining arugula and parmesan on top, as well as pomegranate seeds if you have them. Using a pizza wheel or sharp long knife, cut into six pieces and serve.

WISCONSIN STREET, OCEANSIDE
A Tiny Little Barbecue for 200

Surf legend Donald Takayama, who passed away in 2012, was one of the premier board builders of the last half century. He probably gave away more surfboards to his cadre of protégés, team riders, and friends than anyone in the business. A born entrepreneur, he shaped long and short boards, was a top contest winner from the age of six, ran a retail shop, and even produced Surfer's Choice, a line of his own teriyaki sauce. Donald's talent as a chef was also legendary. In his big backyard in Oceanside, he'd hold barbecues for hundreds. Included below is the secret recipe from his award-winning teriyaki sauce that was once sold in major supermarkets. It's an old family recipe that can't be beat.

Foiled Again
Grilled Fish & Vegetable Packet with Donald Takayama's Teriyaki Sauce

Joel Tudor is perhaps the most elegant and influential longboard stylist of the last two decades. A protégé of Donald Takayama, Joel has carried on Donald's generosity, graciousness, and love of life. This dish has always been a favorite of his and was a staple at Donald's barbecues on Tremont Street in Oceanside. The genius of wrapping the ingredients in foil makes cooking for 200 so much less work—and works just as well for a more intimate dinner.

A classic California swell

SERVES 4

1 cup quartered cherry or grape tomatoes

1 cup diced yellow summer squash

1 cup thinly sliced red onion

¼ cup pitted and coarsely chopped
   Kalamata olives

2 tablespoons fresh lemon juice

1 tablespoon chopped fresh oregano

1 teaspoon capers, rinsed

1½ pounds tilapia fillets, cut into 4
   equal portions

Sea salt and freshly ground pepper, to taste

2 teaspoons slivered fresh garlic

4 teaspoons extra-virgin olive oil

2 tablespoons (more to taste) Donald
   Takayama's Teriyaki Sauce (*recipe follows*)

Light a charcoal grill and bring to medium heat or preheat a gas grill to 350°F.

In a large bowl, combine tomatoes, squash, onion, olives, lemon juice, oregano, and capers. Set aside.

To make a packet, lay out a 20-inch sheet of heavy-duty aluminum foil and coat top of foil with cooking spray. Place one portion of tilapia in center of foil and season to taste with salt and pepper. Top each portion of fish with about 3/4 cup of vegetable mixture and ½ teaspoon garlic. Drizzle each with 1 teaspoon olive oil and 1½ teaspoons teriyaki sauce. Fold foil over, leaving room for steam to gather, and pinch seams to seal tightly. Repeat process with 3 more packets.

Grill packets until fish is cooked through and vegetables are tender, about 5 minutes. Remove from grill and carefully open both ends of packets. Allow steam to escape, and use a spatula to slide contents onto plates. If you're camping or beachside, eat directly out of packet. Or just eat out of packet anyway.

DONALD TAKAYAMA'S TERIYAKI SAUCE

1¼ cups water, divided

5 tablespoons brown sugar

1 clove garlic, minced

Pinch of onion powder

¼ cup pineapple juice

½ teaspoon ground ginger

2 tablespoons cornstarch

Combine 1 cup water, brown sugar, garlic, and onion powder in a small saucepan and cook over medium heat until sugar dissolves. Add pineapple juice and ground ginger and simmer for 10 minutes.

In a small bowl, mix cornstarch with 1/4 cup cold water. Stir into saucepan and continue to simmer until sauce reaches your desired thickness. Add a bit more water if sauce gets too thick for your liking.

All the Pretty Horses

Nursing a longneck Corona at my restaurant, Margarita's Village, Dale Velzy is telling me about riding his *horse* from his family's small coastal ranch to Redondo Beach back in the 1940s. Ranches in Redondo? Wood surfboards strapped to horses?

For years, after he first moved to San Clemente in the early '80s, Dale frequented my restaurant three or four times a week. After a meal at what he called my "joint," he'd often sit for hours telling tales. It was a thrill to have him as a regular.

His customized 1932 little deuce coupe is parked outside. His cowboy hat frames his trademark handlebar mustache as he sets off with a new story. "One night in 1951, I hosted a big beach party. We called it a steak-fry, and we charged three bucks for a huge steak dinner," he says. "All kinds of movie stars showed up—David Niven, Peter Lawford. Movie mogul Daryl Zanuck's daughter Daralyn. A whole bunch of Hollywood starlets. Everybody loved the steaks. But nobody could figure out how we could do it for that price."

I knew a classic ending was coming. Whenever Dale set up a story like this, there'd be a punch line.

Born the year before the great stock market crash of 1929, Dale Velzy was the son of a South Bay boat builder and lifeguard. By age eight he was learning to surf on a homemade board shaped by his father. He did a stint as a rodeo star riding bulls.

At the pinnacle of Dale's success as a surfboard shaper, he ran five surf shops. Filmmaker Bruce Brown had named a North Shore spot Velzyland after Dale bankrolled Brown's first cinematic efforts, which culminated in the landmark movie *The Endless Summer*. It was one of many firsts. Nicknamed Hawk for his sharp eyesight, Dale invented board model names, put the first sticker on a board, and sponsored the first "team rider." Most importantly, in the 1960s, he helped make boards affordable to an all-important customer group: young surfers like me.

Embodying the early California beach ethos, Dale was one lady-charming, hot-rod-driving, tattoo-sporting, fun-loving surf cat, a guy who could ride waves, play music, make surfboards, and barbecue steaks for 200. And one thing was undisputed—no one could top Dale Velzy's barbecues.

"So what happened at the steak-fry, Dale?" I ask. A smile appears under the mustache.

"They were filet mignon medallions. Everybody was raving about the tenderness, the flavor, the cut," he says. "They just wanted to know how we put on a meal like that so cheap." He sits back, taking a long swig off his Corona. No master storyteller can resist a good pause. Dale looks at me and shrugs. "When we announced it was horsemeat, I guess they figured it out."

When Dale Velzy passed away in 2005, his paddle-out memorial at Doheny State Beach in Dana Point was conservatively estimated at 500 participants, making it the largest waterborne ceremony in 100 years of modern surf history. They came from Malibu and Maui, Rincon and Riverside, Cocoa Beach and Koko Head, Australia and Zihuatanejo. There were guys he knew in junior high and guys who were in junior high. If you mentioned his name at the gate, the $15 State Park entry fee was waived in honor of him. That tribute alone speaks for the significance of the man. When the whole damn state of California opens its parking lot for you, *that's* saying something.

Velzy working at his second pasttime

OLD MAN'S, SAN ONOFRE
Playing Real Good for Free

Every September, the Hurley Pro contest takes place at Lower Trestles. Professional surfing events now award hundreds of thousands of dollars in prize money and cost millions to produce. Live webcasts, electronic scoreboards, and instant replays have taken the presentation of the sport to a whole new level. With a big south swell and most of the globe's best professional surfers in attendance, some 5,000 spectators are treated to an extraordinary display of athleticism.

The very weekend that the Hurley Pro's big white tents and scaffolding go up, another contest sets up not more than a mile down the cobbled beach: the San Onofre Surfing Club's annual surf championship, at the break called Old Man's. There's no catered spread, people don't arrive in air-conditioned shuttles, and the show is not produced by a global marketing firm. But the SanO contest, now in its sixth decade, is a wonder to behold.

On the beach that's considered the birthplace of California surf culture, families that have been coming here for four generations drive down the only dirt road left in Southern California where you can still park right at the sand. The food is picnic style; the atmosphere, rich with camaraderie. Surfers from eight to eighty compete in divisions that might have been won by their grandfathers back when the club was founded in 1952. Like Joni Mitchell sang all those years ago, some of the best things in life are free. You won't find finer people, better beach cooking, or a better spirit at any other surf contest. As for the surfing, well, it's not *quite* at the level of the pros at Trestles. But everyone's having fun, and *they play real good for free.*

Roasted Vegetables with Caramelized Balsamic Glaze

This dish can be prepared easily on an outdoor barbecue at the beach and is a lot healthier picnic fare than the typical heap of store-bought macaroni or potato salad slathered in mayonnaise. And it's tastier, too. If you're going to cook on the beach, just chop the vegetables and bring them already marinated to the beach.

SERVES 6

1 red bell pepper

1 orange bell pepper

1 yellow summer squash

1 Japanese eggplant

1 large zucchini

1 large Maui sweet onion

3 tablespoons extra-virgin olive oil

1 teaspoon fresh marjoram

1 tablespoon garlic powder

½ teaspoon crushed fresh rosemary

½ teaspoon chervil

Sea salt and freshly ground pepper, to taste

1 8-ounce bottle balsamic glaze

3 tablespoons brown sugar

1 cup torn or chopped mixed fresh herbs, such as basil, parsley, and rosemary

Light a charcoal grill and bring to medium-high heat or preheat a gas grill to 425°F. Prepare vegetables by slicing lengthwise into 1 x 3-inch pieces, ¼ inch thick. Slice onion into ¼-inch-thick rounds. Place vegetables in large plastic freezer bag, and toss to coat completely with oil, marjoram, garlic powder, rosemary, chervil, salt, and pepper. Let marinate for 30 minutes.

Lay out 2 sheets of heavy-duty aluminum foil on top of each other, large enough to arrange vegetables without crowding. Lightly oil (or spray with cooking spray) top of foil, and place foil sheets on grill. Transfer vegetables to foil and cover with another sheet of foil.

Grill vegetables for 15 to 20 minutes. With metal tongs, turn veggie pieces over and squeeze a little balsamic glaze on each piece. Sprinkle brown sugar over balsamic (to help caramelize it), and grill for another 15 to 20 minutes. Check every 10 minutes for even browning.

With a soft spatula, carefully remove vegetables from foil to a large platter. Sprinkle with fresh herbs and add salt and pepper to taste. If you're picnicking at the beach, skip the platter and serve right off the grill.

51ST STREET, NEWPORT BEACH
Hasta La Pasta

In his under-the-radar fashion, 2016 world champion John John Florence occasionally slips into Newport Beach to talk surfboard design with Bob Hurley, founder of Hurley, John's sponsor brand. Both men have an affinity for fine wave-riding equipment—one as an architect, the other as a test pilot. Bob, a consummate craftsman and business mogul, has shaped many boards for John over the years, and the symbiosis goes far beyond the simple team rider/company owner relationship. They are birds of a feather—humble, soulful, and immensely talented—each with a quiet power most men only dream of.

Pasta Carbonara

World champ John John Florence has a lot of passions: surfing, sailing, skateboarding, snowboarding…and pasta. Carbonara is his favorite, because just about nothing tastes better than eggs, bacon, and a touch of cream tossed with a heaping helping of fresh fettuccine.

   I first encountered this dish many years ago when traveling in Italy. It's now reached the shores of almost every country, because it's so tasty, inexpensive, and versatile—it's a great breakfast, a great dinner, and leftovers are perfect for lunch. It even works as the base of a stir-fry—just add it to stir-fried veggies.

Note: Eating this dish will not make you surf like John John.

SERVES 6

1 pound dried fettuccine
2 tablespoons extra-virgin olive oil
6 slices bacon
5 eggs, lightly beaten
2 tablespoons slivered garlic

1 tablespoon chopped fresh chives
1 teaspoon red pepper flakes
½ teaspoon Italian spice blend
½ cup heavy cream
½ cup chopped fresh parsley (optional)

In a large stockpot, bring 2 quarts water to a boil. Add pasta and oil and cook until just tender, about 8 minutes. Once pasta is done, transfer to colander and drain.

   Place bacon in a skillet and cook over low heat until just crisp, 10 to 12 minutes. Remove bacon from skillet and drain all but 1 tablespoon of bacon fat. Crumble bacon once it's cool enough to handle.

   Over medium-low heat, add eggs to skillet and cook, scrambling, until eggs are just cooked but still slightly runny. Return pasta to skillet, tossing to let eggs coat pasta, about 2 minutes. Add garlic, chives, red pepper flakes, and spice blend. Gradually stir in crumbled bacon and cream. Toss all ingredients until eggs are cooked through and cream is absorbed into pasta, about 3 minutes.

   Serve directly from skillet or on individual plates, and top with parsley if you like.

MAVERICKS, HALF MOON BAY
Mavericks of Mavericks

The utter scale of Mavericks—the rugged cliffs, the foamy outside peak that reaches forty feet, and the rocks in between—makes for one of California's epic seascapes.

From its naming in 1991 after a German shepherd named Maverick to Jeff Clark's lonely decade-and-a-half solo surf sessions; from its strange-shaped underwater rock formation to its tragic—even mysterious—drownings, Mavericks is the stuff of legends. It changed the way big-wave surfing was perceived and brought Hawaiian big-wave experts to California, where they met a fearless band of local titans who redefined the act of big-wave riding in dangerous conditions.

The recipe here is in honor of all those mavericks who have taken off on waves at this monster spot. For those who took their last wave there—and those who came too close—this is a humble salute to you.

Half Moon Bay Salad
Crab, Artichoke, Avocado & Pistachio Salad with Lime Cilantro Dressing

In the little Pillar Point Harbor just across the channel from Mavericks, the fishing boats bring in some of the best crab in California. This recipe is a classic salad preparation using an entire set of California ingredients. Each of these towns claims to produce the highest quality for their specialty: avocados from Fallbrook, artichoke hearts from Castroville, garlic from Gilroy, pistachios from Fresno, butter lettuce from Santa Barbara, tomatoes from Ojai, goat cheese from Sonoma, and crab caught just off the coast near Mavericks.

SERVES 6

2 cups crabmeat, picked over and cleaned

2 tablespoons light mayonnaise

½ teaspoon Dijon mustard

6 artichoke hearts, cut into half moons

3 cups coarsely chopped butter lettuce

1 large ripe avocado, cut lengthwise into ¼-inch slices, like half moons

3 small ripe tomatoes, quartered into half moons

½ cup shelled pistachios (about 24)

3 ounces soft goat cheese, divided into 12 small half-moon sections

3 tablespoons fresh lime juice

2 tablespoons fruity extra-virgin olive oil

1 tablespoon avocado oil

2 tablespoons finely chopped fresh cilantro

1 tablespoon finely chopped fresh parsley

3 cloves roasted garlic, mashed

½ teaspoon cumin

1 tablespoon chives, snipped in ½-inch pieces

1 teaspoon freshly ground pepper

2 crab legs and claws, for garnish (optional)

Combine crabmeat, mayonnaise, and mustard in a small bowl. Mix well and set aside.

In a large salad bowl, combine artichoke hearts, lettuce, avocado, tomatoes, pistachios, and goat cheese. Add crab mixture and toss gently to combine.

In a small bowl, combine lime juice, olive oil, avocado oil, cilantro, parsley, garlic, and cumin and whisk until smooth. Drizzle dressing over salad and toss again until dressing coats lettuce. Sprinkle with chives and pepper, and serve. For a splurge, garnish with crab legs and claws.

Photo next page: Golden Mavericks—power, size, and grandeur that was undiscovered for fifty years

MARGARITA'S VILLAGE, SAN CLEMENTE
My Very Best Bogart

The restaurant business produces some interesting rituals. One is the customer's desire to have a personal connection with the owner. (The same is true with surf shops and shapers.) One night at my restaurant, a couple ran up a food and bar bill of several hundred dollars. Afterward, they asked to meet me. I was playing the part of the suave restaurateur—on Saturday nights I wore a taupe-white linen suit cut in a 1940s style. Forgive me, but it was the '80s—*Miami Vice* was all the rage. I sauntered over and introduced myself.

"It's so wonderful to meet you! The food is to die for!" Well dressed and effervescent, the elegant woman spoke with a slightly overbearing self-confidence. Obviously from Newport Beach. "When we found out you had won two Food Critics' awards, we just *had* to come down. What a fabulous place! Palms, real Mexican art—it's like being in Puerto Vallarta!"

They carried on, and I knew my job was to smile a lot and tell them how happy I was that they were there.

"And look at you, that suit!" She was over the top now. "You look just like Humphrey Bogart in *Casablanca*!" I don't care how humble a restaurant owner tries to be, this kind of talk will make anyone puff up a little. I finally excused myself, saying that I needed to check on their dessert. "Oh," she cooed, "you're probably going back to have a romantic moonlight drink with Ingrid Bergman!" I saw no reason to dim the gleam of her illusion. The fact that the kitchen was a chaotic cauldron and my wife looked more like Ava Gardner was of no matter.

I strolled back toward the kitchen. The dining room was full, there was a ninety-minute wait, the bar was overflowing, and I'd just received a head-swelling rave from big-spending new patrons. How much better could it get?

In the kitchen, I headed to check on their dessert, handmade by our Guadalajara-born pastry chef, Victoria.

And then the kitchen blew up.

The long rubber power-wash hose by the dishwashing station suddenly ruptured. The tiny puncture shot out scalding, highly pressurized steam. It hit the dishwasher in the face and he went down, dropping the hose's handle as he fell. The spewing spray hit the central grill, which exploded in grease-fueled flames. Line cooks dove away from the inferno, colliding with a dishwashing table piled high with dirty dishes, sending them crashing across the floor. The rubber hose spun crazily, hitting the grill every three seconds or so, creating more eruptions. Cooks and prep staff ducked under any cover, many falling onto the floor.

In desperation, I charged the hose, slipping twice on the mess on the tile floor. It was like charging a machine gun that had been mowing your troops down. Better to face the fire now with a chance of survival than stand there and know death was certain.

As the tube sprayed me across the chest, I grabbed the hose and sealed off the spewing leak with my hands. "*Cerrado la agua!* Shut the water valve!" I yelled. Palms scalded, I plunged the hose into the rinse sink filled with cold water, falling across the muck on the dish table. *Cerrado la agua!*

A cook scurried on all fours from under a table and twisted the water main, stopping the pressure. Someone else shut off the fire alarm. Soot blanketed the kitchen, and thirty dinners lay sprawled across the grease-splattered floor. The staff was already mopping and washing.

It was, mercifully, a self-contained disaster. Thanks to our heavy steel kitchen fire doors, the diners never knew anything was amiss. We'd take a hit in revenue, be late with a dozen dinner orders, and have lots of cleanup. And my linen suit was a sopping, dirty dishrag.

Still, I had to smile. Back in the dining room, that Newport Beach couple was imagining me having a romantic cocktail with Ingrid Bergman.

Winter California migration: birds, swell, and beach sand

Quesadilla Kempton

This was the best-selling appetizer at Margarita's Village. It's easy to make and almost decadent in its flavor.

MAKES 3 QUESADILLAS

1 pound chorizo (Carmelita brand preferred)
6 tablespoons extra-virgin olive oil, divided
18 mushrooms, thinly sliced
3 green onions, sliced in 1/4-inch rounds
6 large flour tortillas

8 ounces mixed Mexican cheeses—such as Chihuahua, Asadero, and Oaxaca (you can substitute jack and mild cheddar), finely shredded
6 tablespoons sour cream
1 small avocado, cut into 12 thin slices
1 tomato, diced

In a medium frying pan, cook chorizo on medium-low heat until browned and cooked through, about 20 minutes, stirring frequently. Discard liquid fat and set chorizo aside.

In a small skillet, heat 3 tablespoons oil over medium heat and sauté mushrooms and onions until just soft, about 5 minutes. Remove from heat and reserve in a bowl.

Add 1 tablespoon olive oil to a 10-inch pan over medium heat, and place a tortilla in the pan. Spread a large dollop of chorizo over whole tortilla, and spread ⅓ of mushroom-onion mixture evenly over chorizo. Top with about 2 ounces of Mexican cheese, and place a second tortilla on top of mixture. Fry for about 2 minutes, then turn over with a spatula and cook for 2 minutes on other side until slightly browned.

Remove from pan and let sit for 2 minutes. Cut into 8 slices with a pizza wheel or large chef's knife. Repeat the process with the remaining tortillas and ingredients, adding a little more oil each time as needed.

When you're ready to serve, drop 2 tablespoons of sour cream in the center of each quesadilla and top with avocado and diced tomato.

Surfwise Steel-Cut Oatmeal

Steel-cut oats are a power food because they're an excellent source of protein, soluble and insoluble fiber, and select vitamins and minerals. The benefits of steel-cut oats exceed the benefits of rolled oats because of the way they are processed.

You can also get this breakfast at San Clemente Café in San Clemente or Beach Break Café in Oceanside, both on Pacific Coast Highway, both major SoCal surf cafés.

SERVES 1

1½ cups water
2 tablespoons dried cherries
½ cup steel-cut oats
½ cup skim milk
½ cup coarsely chopped glazed pecans

½ banana, thinly sliced
2 tablespoons fresh blueberries
2 tablespoons maple syrup
1 tablespoon shredded coconut

Bring water to a boil in a medium saucepan. Spoon 2 tablespoons of the boiling water into a cup, and let the dried cherries soak in it to soften.

Stir oats into pan of boiling water and reduce heat to low. Cook until oats are done to your liking, about 12 minutes, stirring frequently to prevent burning on bottom.

Remove from heat, mix in cherries and all other ingredients, and chow down!

OLD MAN'S, SAN ONOFRE

Surfwise & Pound Foolish:
The Paskowitz Family's Astounding Saga

Most surfers know the story of Doc Paskowitz: Stanford Medical School grad falls in love with surfing, falls in love with Julia, sires nine children, decides the medical profession is not his life path, moves the family into an oversized camper, and spends the next twenty-five years living (and helping to invent) the surfing bohemian lifestyle as the whole family travels together along America's beaches, operating the first overnight surf camps. If this sounds like a made-for-Hollywood screenplay, it was. The 2007 documentary film *Surfwise* chronicled the Paskowitz family saga and earned overwhelmingly positive reviews and a short but brilliant theatrical run.

The story, as might be imagined, runs much deeper than that, including when it comes to food. Doc Paskowitz wrote a regular health column for me in *Surfer* during my editorship, and I became good friends with the family, watching the kids grow up at San Onofre State Beach. A health fanatic, Doc wrote the book *Surfing and Health*, which is a great read. Oatmeal, of course, was one of the breakfast staples. "It was more like the gruel served in *David Copperfield*," recalls Jonathan, the second son and family bon vivant. "We hated it, but it was part of the strict low-fat, low-sugar diet my dad demanded. It was also low cost," he says, laughing.

Doc was right and so is Jonathan: Oatmeal is a great healthy food, solid as a bass guitar—but it needs other instruments to make it soar into a chart-topping meal. In Doc's honor, I came up with this oatmeal in an effort to create a symphony from a simple folk song. It's got all the nutrients you need to start your day—and it also has flavor. The Paskowitz family loves it. Like I love them.

San Onofre, the birthplace of Southern California surf culture

CENTRAL AMERICA
Crossroads of Latin Flavors

During my eight years as the media director at Billabong USA, I also managed the brand's surf-camp program. I added a "Surf with a Pro" component that brought top pro surfers on a safari with surf camp clients to a premier surf break. Wave riders who attended one of these trips got to spend a week with a legend and get some coaching as well. For everyday surfers it was a peak experience. Our most frequent destinations were in Central America, often at surf resorts with dining right on the beach.

I was fortunate enough to have yet another "professional" reason to explore Centro's surf breaks and cuisine, as the director of Quiksilver's Crossing Project, which sent a rotating cast of surfers, photographers, and even researchers on surf explorations around the world aboard a reconditioned trawler called the *Indies Trader.*

For such a small part of the world, Central America has an enormous diversity of surf. Nicaragua is almost entirely long stretches of offshore beach breaks, while neighboring El Salvador is the land of the points. Panama's Caribbean coast harbors waves that get over fifteen feet, and Costa Rica provides river-mouth and cobblestone setups.

Centro cuisine is equally diverse: It's a profusion of Latin flavors, with each country contributing a distinctive national dish. Fresh, colorful, and tropical, Central American food is healthy and satisfying.

Dylan Graves tastes the Nicaraguan sea life on the Indies Trader.

Catalina, Panama—a big, heavy wave in a small, friendly country

Blackened Corvina with Garlic Mushroom Sauce 90

Mariscada 95
Salvadoran Seafood Soup

Nicaraguan Macuá Cocktail 97

Caliche's Wishbone Grilled Lobster with Coconut Mojo 98

Arroz con Pollo 101
Rice with Chicken & Vegetables

Costa Rican Coffee-Rubbed Pork with Marmalade Glaze 102

Smoky Corn Salsa 105

Grilled Asparagus with Crab Chipotle Mayonnaise 107

For sale: Seafood! Shrimp! Fish fillets!

Blackened Corvina with Garlic Mushroom Sauce

Bob "Don Roberto" Rotherham discovered one of the world's best point breaks in El Salvador, married a local woman, and built a life around his passion. He had the surf to himself during the Sandinista civil war and has enough stories to fill Wikipedia. Nowadays, he holds court at his little restaurant, one of the most popular in El Salvador, entertaining his guests with tales of the perils of the tropics. His son Jimmy is a world-class surfer who could have competed on the pro tour if he wasn't busy piloting planes and dominating his home break. When the *Indies Trader* sailed its Central American leg, Jimmy traveled with us and was everyone's favorite passenger.

Everyone also loves Bob's signature dish at the restaurant: a lavish but simple-to-cook blackened corvina with garlic mushroom sauce. A Centro fish often called white sea bass, corvina has a mild, sweet taste with firm, large-flaked flesh. This dish should not be eaten without a cold Suprema Premium lager or appropriate cocktail.

SERVES 6

3 tablespoons sweet paprika

1½ tablespoons garlic salt

1½ tablespoons dried thyme

1½ teaspoons chopped fresh rosemary

1 teaspoon freshly ground black pepper

1 teaspoon minced red chile pepper

3 tablespoons unsalted butter

6 corvina (white sea bass) fillets

Garlic Mushroom Sauce (*recipe follows*)

3 tablespoons minced fresh dill

6 lemon wedges

Light a charcoal grill and bring to medium heat or preheat a gas grill to 350°F.

In a bowl, combine paprika, garlic salt, thyme, rosemary, black pepper, and red chile pepper to create a spice rub. Melt the butter and pour into a separate bowl. Dip each piece of fish in butter and sprinkle it with spice mixture.

Place fish fillets on a well-oiled grill pan, set on hot grill, and cook for 3 to 4 minutes. Turn fish carefully with a spatula and cook 3 to 4 minutes on other side. Fish should have a burnished, blackened look. Place fish on a large serving plate, spoon Garlic Mushroom Sauce over top, add a sprinkle of dill, and serve with lemon wedges.

GARLIC MUSHROOM SAUCE

2 tablespoons extra-virgin olive oil

1 tablespoon unsalted butter

6 cloves garlic, chopped (about ½ cup)

2 cups thinly sliced mushrooms of your choice

2 tablespoons chopped fresh parsley

1 tablespoon white wine or brandy

3 tablespoons heavy cream

In a medium pan, heat olive oil and butter on low heat. Add garlic and sauté until golden, about 1 minute. Add mushrooms, parsley, and wine, and cook for 3 minutes without stirring. Gently stir in cream and simmer until sauce thickens slightly, about 5 minutes. Keep warm until needed.

TAMARINDO, COSTA RICA

Almost Across the River and Into the Trees

"Let us cross over the river and rest under the shade of the trees."

—The last words of legendary Confederate general Stonewall Jackson,
who died in a tragic miscalculation on a moonless night

On the coast near Nicoya, rivers run down to the Pacific Ocean and empty onto sandy beaches with thin, peaky waves. The water upstream is muddy and slow moving; snake-like dirt roads slither along barren networks of dried mud flats.

Driving one of these roads for the last hour in darkness, our path had turned into a rutted track lined with murky swamps. There was no moon. At the third river crossing, we stopped. The bridge had been washed out.

Our headlights showed that the river was nearly waist deep; it would come up to our car doors. It looked wet but not overly dangerous—the current was slow and the ford was only thirty yards across. We had two solid Land Rovers. One could pull the other across if necessary. We could cross and camp in the shelter of the grove of trees we saw on the other side; there looked to be enough deadwood for a fire. Or we could turn back toward the last town we'd passed a few hours earlier. `

We decided to go ahead, easing the vehicles down the hard, pebble-strewn embankment, ready to wade alongside them. Just as the first Land Rover reached the water's edge, an old man with a lantern appeared. He'd run all the way from his little shack nearly 200 yards away. He was panting a little, his legs somewhat bowed but sturdy from a lifetime of labor. *Hold back,* he told us in Spanish. *Don't try to cross the river.*

Okay, our best Spanish speaker said. *Why? Is the road washed out? The mud too thick?*

The old man shook his head. He held up his lantern and turned toward the water. After staring for a few moments, he pointed. "Cocodrilos," he said. "Grandes."

Now we saw it—the beast was as long as a stretch limo, with hind haunches the size of tractor wheels. He was idling, a flat, log-like form parallel to the stream bank, just behind where we were about to rumble through the murky waterway. As the old man focused his light, the green glimmer of a reptilian eye met our gaze—a man-eater whose prey had almost come right to the dinner table.

The old man pointed again. "Alli." *There.* Just beyond the view of our headlights were two more, lying as still as the shadows that hid their cross-hatched waffle skin.

We nodded to the old man and got back in the vehicles. He motioned us up the slope to camp out in his ramshackle yard. His wife gave us cold empanadas and warm Fanta to wipe the brassy taste of fear still burbling out of our throats. It would be a long night. But our luck had been better than that of the character in *Across the River and Into the Trees,* Hemingway's famous novel. And better than Stonewall Jackson's, too. A human talisman had come out of his shelter in the dead of night to warn total strangers who were about to wade headlong across the river and into the trees.

Waiting for dinner across the river

LAS FLORES, EL SALVADOR
Mango Point Potage

One of our favorite Billabong "Surf with a Pro" surf-camp destinations was Las Flores
in El Salvador. Posh and isolated, it holds two excellent point breaks—the wave out front and
Punta Mango, a ten-minute boat ride up the coast—along with luxurious (by camping standards)
accommodations. To top it off, the chef back then could really cook. One of his most popular dishes
was Mariscada Salvadorena, a seafood-packed soup that's a national dish. The chef was kind enough
to share his recipe with me.

Mariscada
Salvadoran Seafood Soup

One of my regular pros on these trips was Donavon Frankenreiter, who's turned a youthful surf career into an astonishingly successful musical career. He's one of the funniest, zaniest, most talented cats I know. Most days after a lunch of this soup, Donny would play a set, the highlight of the afternoon.

I like to serve this soup with a mango salad, in honor of the great Punta Mango wave, the great chef who made this version, and the great crew at the resort.

SERVES 6

⅓ cup extra-virgin olive oil, divided
½ cup chopped white onion
½ cup finely chopped flat-leaf parsley
¼ cup finely diced carrots
¼ cup finely diced celery
¼ cup finely diced red bell pepper
3 teaspoons minced garlic
6 littleneck clams, washed
3 tablespoons flour
1 lobster tail, cleaned and chopped into about 6 bite-size pieces
24 medium shrimp, peeled and deveined

6 large diver scallops, halved
¼ cup dry sherry
6 mussels, washed
8 ounces calamari pieces (fresh or frozen)
2 tablespoons unsalted butter
1 tablespoon red pepper flakes
1 tablespoon slivered garlic
3 cups vegetable broth
1 cup fish stock
½ cup heavy cream
3 tablespoons snipped chives
Sea salt and freshly ground pepper, to taste

Place a large pot over medium heat and add 2 tablespoons olive oil. Add onion, parsley, carrots, celery, bell pepper, and garlic, and sauté for 3 minutes. Stir in clams and sauté another 5 minutes.

Using a spoon, push the clams and vegetables to one side. Sprinkle flour onto the bottom of the pot and stir to make a thin, smooth roux. Add lobster and shrimp, and cook for 1 minute over medium heat. Add scallops and cook for 2 minutes more to sear the scallops. With a slotted spoon, transfer all the seafood to a bowl and set aside.

Pour sherry into the pot and, one at a time, add mussels and calamari. Stir and then add back reserved seafood. Simmer until sherry evaporates, about 3 minutes. Add butter, red pepper flakes, and garlic slivers. Pour in vegetable broth and fish stock. Bring to a boil and simmer until mussels and clams are fully opened, about 4 minutes, and shrimp and scallops are opaque, about 2 minutes more.

Lower heat; stir heavy cream into mixture, heating for 2 minutes more, and let sit off heat for 20 minutes, which will help the flavors meld.

When ready to serve, gently reheat and carefully ladle mixture into 6 bowls, making sure some of each type of seafood is included in each bowl. Garnish with chives, and season to taste with salt and pepper.

PUNTA BRUJA, NICARAGUA
The Witching Hour

The national forest that covers the border of Costa Rica and Nicaragua has iguanas the size of jackrabbits. It's also a breeding ground for bushmaster pit vipers, the largest and most aggressive snake in the southern Americas. They're joined by cougars, crocodiles, and banana spiders, the most poisonous insect on the planet. It keeps your eyes open.

We'd only seen the iguanas, but we heard the high-pitched call of the rare bird called *pajaro macuá* clear and sharp from the treetops. We were searching for a fabled surf spot, Punta Bruja— Witch's Rock—thinking maybe the forest (or one of those snakes) had swallowed it up. With no maps to help, we just kept going. The jungle got dense and the road got worse.

Friends had told me about this kind of exploration: vehicles sinking to their bumpers in mud. Or rolling over on a steep grade. We were driving on boulders as big as our Jeep. Rains had washed out sections of the road on the cliff; we crept forward one wheel at a time. We could have used a good macuá cocktail by the time we got to the bottom of the cliff two hours later.

The panorama spread out before us. The river emerged from the canyon we'd spent the early afternoon driving down, forming an enormous, beautiful sandbar delta. Out beyond, a solitary four-story rock stood straight out of the ocean like a massive black granite domino, smooth on the sides and flat on top. Time and tides had cut three diagonal slices in the monolith.

Our footsteps across the wet, silver sand sent thousands of undulating patterns across the expanse. The sensation was mystic, almost majestic. We were completely alone. Then the wind began. Through the slices in the rock rose an eerie, high-pitched whistle. The waves thundered, whipped to shapelessness by the wind. It was unnerving.

With the sun going low and the wind coming high, we decided our best choice was to make it back to the nearest village by dark. The villagers called it the "magic rock" and told us to try again another day. "*Esta perfecto,*" they said. We waited and went back when the conditions were right. And it was.

Witch's Rock letting its veil blow from its face

Nicaraguan Macuá Cocktail

This drink's name comes from an elusive tropical forest bird that's native to Nicaragua. Legend has it that the pajaro macuá has magical properties that attract beautiful women. Men have been known to rub the feathers of this bird on their chests as an aphrodisiac.

Created by Dr. Edmundo Sáenz from Granada, this drink won the title of Nicaraguan National Cocktail in a 2006 competition. The ingredients are all staples of Nicaragua: tropical fruits, outstanding rum, and pure cane sugar.

Note: Do not attempt to attract women by rubbing this cocktail on your chest.

MAKES 1 COCKTAIL

3 ounces white Flor de Caña rum
3 ounces guava juice
1½ ounces fresh lime juice

Light brown sugar, to taste
1 cup crushed ice
1 lemon or orange slice, for garnish

Blend rum, juices, and sugar with ice, and pour into a highball glass. Garnish the glass with the citrus slice and serve immediately.

JACÓ, COSTA RICA

Caliche's Wishbone Grilled Lobster with Coconut Mojo

Costa Rica's unofficial surf ambassador, Caliche Alfaro, owns Caliche's Wishbone, a popular restaurant in Jacó and hangout for traveling surfers. Gilbert Brown, the irrepressible, dreadlocked four-time Costa Rican national champion, frequents this soulful food establishment, along with Kelly Slater, Rob Machado, and Julian Wilson. Caliche's signature dish is lobster, and this version is Julian's favorite.

SERVES 8, or 4 if you're hungry

COCONUT MOJO

4 teaspoons light virgin olive oil

Zest of 1 lemon

1 teaspoon turmeric

¼ cup water

4 red chile peppers, roasted

½ cup diced green onions, white and green parts divided

2 tablespoons slivered fresh garlic

2 cans coconut milk

1 cup shredded coconut

½ cup tarragon leaves, torn into 1-inch pieces

½ cup chopped cilantro

¼ cup orange juice

1 tablespoon grated fresh ginger

LOBSTER

1 cup (2 sticks) unsalted butter, melted

4 large lobster tails, cleaned and split in halves

Sea salt and freshly ground black pepper, to taste

To make the Coconut Mojo, heat oil in a 10-inch skillet over medium heat. Add lemon zest, turmeric, and water. Reduce heat to low and simmer for 20 minutes to let lemon infuse. After 15 minutes, add chiles and diced white parts of green onions. After 3 more minutes, add garlic and continue simmering for the final 2 minutes.

While lemon zest mixture is simmering, pour coconut milk into a saucepan over low heat. Add shredded coconut, green parts of green onion, tarragon, cilantro, orange juice, and ginger, and stir together. Simmer until mixture begins to thicken slightly, about 10 minutes.

Add lemon zest oil mixture to coconut milk mixture and stir well to combine. Set sauce aside until needed. You can make this up to 2 days in advance and store in the fridge.

To make the lobster, light a charcoal grill and bring to medium-high heat or preheat a gas grill to 375°F. While it's heating up, take a brush and coat lobster with butter, and add salt and pepper to taste.

Place lobsters on grill, split side down. Grill lobsters, basting regularly with butter, for about 6 minutes, then turn over to shell side and continue to baste with butter until flesh turns white and firm to touch, about another 6 minutes. Be careful not to overcook.

Arrange lobster on a serving platter and spoon some of the Mojo sauce over the top. Provide a bowl or small pitcher of remaining sauce for guests to add as they wish.

CANAL ZONE, PANAMA
Canal Zoning

It's a strange thing to watch a seven-story oil tanker disappear. Standing on the Miraflores dock midway across the Panama Canal, that's exactly what you see. Twenty-five million gallons of water drain away as vessels begin their descent in the lock, and shortly afterward, eighty-two-foot gates open below. Deck by deck, the massive cargo ship lowers beneath the dock until there is nothing to see but the other side of the canal.

Remarkably, ships require only two feet of clearance on each side of the canal itself. In the Canal Zone, the *Indies Trader* was the midget on the block—a seventy-five-foot, ninety-five-ton salvage vessel that looked more like a tugboat than an exploration yacht. Each time it passed through the canal, we were slotted in with a mammoth cargo ship, like a mouse sitting next to an elephant. The schedulers would wedge the *Trader* in the space between its enormous companion and the lock walls. In this 110-foot-wide area, our little cracker box traversed the Canal Zone, squeezed next to an eighty-foot-wide, 965-foot-long cargo ship.

Vessels transit through three locks, a rain forest, and a man-made lake, then down three locks on the other side before exiting into a different ocean. It's a trip worth every nickel and every minute it takes. Each of the four times we passed through this giant watery stepladder, I was astonished at the scale and mass of the engineering. It is a wonder of the world.

We stocked up on snacks, since you can't cook much while traversing the canal. My favorite was the scrumptious, if not exactly healthy, Panamanian cinnamon rolls. They're tedious to make, and taste just as good when bought from the little stands on the street.

ISLA COIBA, PANAMA
Fanta, Santa & Fantasies

In the US, almost no one drinks Fanta. But in Central America, it's as ubiquitous as Coca-Cola is here, with signs and wall posters everywhere.

In most of Central America, almost no one celebrates Santa Claus. In Costa Rica, the baby Jesus brings gifts on the night before Christmas. In Nicaragua, all-night caroling starts the season, along with processions carrying statues of the Virgin Mary. In Panama, boat parades, marching bands, tree lightings, and costumed dancers fill the squares. In El Salvador, it's midnight Mass and fireworks.

Every Central American country has its own traditions. All, however, have one holiday custom in common: feasting. Chicken, turkey, rice, and lots of sweets fill the table. In every country, these lavish dinners always include tamales, and they are a fantasy worth trying. But they're a lot of work. Instead, consider this festive, colorful, one-dish meal of chicken, rice, and vegetables as a great dish for the holidays—or any other time. Not only is it tasty, but it's so healthy that you won't feel guilty about slugging down a couple of bottles of Fanta.

Arroz con Pollo
Rice with Chicken & Vegetables

SERVES 6

10 cloves garlic, crushed

1 tablespoon achiote powder

1 tablespoon ground cumin

1½ teaspoons ground coriander

Sea salt, to taste

2½ pounds boneless, skinless chicken breasts, each cut in half

2 to 3 tablespoons oil or melted unsalted butter

1 white onion, diced (about 2 cups)

6 firm medium tomatoes, quartered

1 green bell pepper, diced

2 medium carrots, diced

2 celery stalks, diced

2 cups jasmine long-grain rice

1 cup Dos Equis Amber or other beer

1 cup chicken broth

1 cup peas, fresh or frozen

1 tablespoon turmeric (this will turn your rice a beautiful golden yellow)

3 tablespoons finely chopped cilantro

Sea salt and freshly ground pepper, to taste

Fried plantains (optional)

Avocado slices (optional)

In a bowl, mix crushed garlic, achiote, cumin, coriander, and salt. Rub garlic seasoning all over chicken pieces.

Heat oil or butter over medium-high heat in a large sauté pan, add chicken pieces, and sear until browned, about 3 minutes per side. Transfer to a platter and set aside.

In the same pan, sauté diced onion, tomatoes, bell pepper, carrots, and celery for 5 minutes, stirring frequently. Add rice, beer, chicken broth, peas, turmeric, and reserved chicken pieces. Stir all ingredients well, then cover and cook over low heat for about 20 minutes.

Reduce heat to very low, uncover, and simmer for an additional 5 minutes, or until rice is tender. Stir in chopped cilantro, and season to taste.

Transfer to a platter. To make it even better, you can surround the chicken and rice with fried plantains and top with avocado slices. Serve with a fresh salad.

Costa Rican Coffee-Rubbed Pork with Marmalade Glaze

This recipe needs a quick cook over high heat and then a few minutes over low heat. Pork tenderloins are very lean and should not be overcooked or they'll get dry and chewy, so keep your eye on the meat thermometer.

Note: Cerveza Imperial, which happens to be Costa Rica's best beer, has been declared "water positive," meaning it helps conserve and clean the water—a very cool thing. Support their efforts: Have an Imperial while you grill. And while you eat. And after you're done. And...

SERVES 6

SPICE RUB

3 tablespoons freshly ground Costa Rican coffee

1 tablespoon sea salt

1 tablespoon sweet paprika

1 tablespoon dark brown sugar

1 teaspoon freshly ground black pepper

1 teaspoon garlic powder

1 teaspoon onion powder

PORK

1 cup orange marmalade

2 teaspoons Grand Marnier

1 teaspoon triple sec or Cointreau

1 teaspoon soy sauce

2 pork tenderloins, about 2 pounds each

2 teaspoons extra-virgin olive oil

Combine ground coffee, salt, paprika, brown sugar, pepper, and garlic and onion powders in a small bowl, and mix well; set aside.

In another small bowl, combine marmalade, Grand Marnier, triple sec, and soy sauce and mix well; set aside.

Trim pork of any silver skin and pat it dry with paper towels. Using your hands, rub tenderloins all over with oil and then spice rub, until evenly coated. Let tenderloins sit at room temperature for at least 30 minutes before grilling.

When it's time to cook, heat a gas grill to medium (350° to 425°F). Oil the grill grates and place tenderloins on grill. Cover and cook, turning every 3 minutes, until tenderloins are browned all over and an instant-read thermometer inserted into thickest part registers 120°F, about 6 minutes. Reduce grill heat to low and brush on half of marmalade glaze. Continue cooking on low until internal temperature reaches 135°F, about 5 more minutes. Remove from heat and brush with remaining marmalade glaze.

Transfer tenderloins to a cutting board, cover with foil, and let rest for 10 minutes. The internal temperature should rise to 145°F. Cut crosswise into 1/2-inch-thick slices and serve.

BOCA BARRANCA, COSTA RICA
Don't Mention It

There was a time when traveling surfers heeded the code "Take only photos, leave only footprints" and never identified a specific surfing spot.

On a *Surfer* magazine trip to Costa Rica once, we surfed long, head-high peelers at Boca Barranca before there was anything else there. Just shacks along the beach and one hotel. Surfing after 10 a.m. required rolling off your board frequently to keep from overheating—the water is just too warm to be refreshing.

Out of the surf we headed for Gary's snack shop just off the beach. By the time we got there, we were bone-dry, salt already beginning to itch. Fresh, ice-cold coconut milk and a paper plate of rice and beans with an egg on top hit the spot. "There are a few of us who've been living down here quite a few years now," Gary said. "We'd sure hate to see the place get overrun."

"I've been shooting spots for a long time," said Jeff Divine, the photographer on the trip. "I've never burned a place yet."

"Don't give it another thought," I added. "They won't even know what country it's in."

Gary gave us the lowdown on where to find good waves and where the crocodiles hang—either trying to be helpful or scare us witless (actually, it was both). He told us to come back that evening and try his coffee-rubbed pork. When we finished our lunch, we thanked him for the food, the info, and the trust. "Don't mention it," he said graciously. As we walked away, he called out, *"And don't MENTION it."*

We kept the location to ourselves, but the rest of the world didn't. Where mangroves once stretched for miles, now man groves cluster on every beach. Time and tide changes.

Street vendors sharing a great cuisine

CORINTO, NICARAGUA
Fixing a Hole

At the end of the rainy season the *Indies Trader* set out from the industrial port of Corinto, down the northern Nicaraguan coast, exploring for surf. On the first night we anchored a safe distance from the shoreline, far outside of the swell line. We'd passed no vessels on the way and had lost radio contact with the port, and for the last twenty miles had seen no sign of human activity along the coast—we were alone.

In the morning, our captain, Martin, and I started the outboard motorboat and headed down the coast on a reconnaissance mission, looking for waves. Within an hour our little fourteen-foot aluminum vessel came across a stunning sight: a large outer-reef bombora with a hollow, pitching inside ledge. It looked a lot like Pipeline—shallow, close to shore, and barreling. Martin pulled inside the channel of the inside break to get a closer look. Like every good captain, he wanted to get a fix on the spot. When the wave was a hollow one, he called it fixing a hole.

We watched as wave after wave hit the ledge, threw out, formed a tube, and spit with fury as it closed. We stood mesmerized by the power and perfection. The second set was already breaking over the inside ledge when we glanced outside. Out on the bombora were huge swell lines to the horizon. We were caught inside with a set of twelve-foot waves heading straight for us.

"Hang on," Martin said. There was nothing to hang on to—just the steering column and the knee-high rails of the boat. He gunned the engine and popped over the first wave without slowing. By the time we were on the fourth wave, he had to throttle back, ease up the face, and drop over the back side.

An aluminum OBM is a fine craft, a step up from the fiberglass skiffs that can shatter from a big wave's impact or the pangas that can swamp in heavy seas. But it's no match for a twelve-foot set breaking on a shallow outer reef. The sixth wave was feathering and lurching, and we knew we'd have to punch it. "Hang on," Martin said in a level tone. We slammed into the wave at full speed, busted through the top of the lip, and entered the space between ocean and air where sea vessels do not belong. The reentry impact threw us sprawling across the ribbed bottom of the boat. After a slight blackout period, I saw a red stream spurt from my kneecap. It was small but pressurized—in perfect sync with my heartbeat, about as big as a pencil lead and spurting about three inches high per heartbeat.

"You've got a hole in your knee." Martin was stating an obvious fact.

He tied off my leg, and we started back to the *Indies Trader*. The ride was bumpy. When my head wasn't swimming from the sight of the water in the floor deck turning a deeper pink, it was spinning from confronting my situation. We were out of radio contact with the *Indies Trader* and more than an hour away from it. The *Trader* was out of radio contact with the port authorities and two hours from the harbor—which was not the place to get medical help. Getting seriously hurt out here, or losing the outboard motor, had never occurred to me.

By the time we reached the *Trader*, the bleeding had subsided. Wound cleaned, it was nothing more than a deep puncture, probably from impact with a screw bolt. By evening the rain came in, and the *Trader* was moving again. We didn't know it yet, but on our return a few weeks later that wave would produce two *Surfer* covers. I made time for a number of things that weren't important yesterday. A crew member had fixed the hole in my knee, Martin had a fix on the hole in the newly discovered wave, and the chef had fixed a fabulous dinner. I ate it slowly, carefully—to keep my mind from wandering.

Smoky Corn Salsa

I don't remember what the main course was for dinner that night—my foot was elevated and I eased the hole-in-my-knee pain with some good mojitos. I do remember this salsa, though, and have made it ever since when I need a little comfort. This is terrific with the Blackened Corvina (*see page 90*) or any grilled fish dish.

SERVES 6, as a topping

4 tablespoons extra-virgin olive oil, divided
1 red bell pepper, diced
1 green bell pepper, diced
4 cups cooked fresh corn kernels
1 bunch green onions, diced
2 cloves garlic, minced

1 teaspoon ground cumin
2 tablespoons fresh lime juice
1 tablespoon bottled chipotle hot sauce
$2/3$ cup chopped fresh cilantro

Heat 2 tablespoons oil in a large skillet over medium-high heat. Add bell peppers and corn, and sauté, stirring occasionally, for about 7 minutes. Add green onions and cook for another 3 minutes. Stir in garlic and cumin, and cook until garlic becomes aromatic, about 2 minutes.

Transfer to serving bowl and stir in lime juice, remaining olive oil, and hot sauce. Let cool. Sprinkle with cilantro and serve.

PANAMA CITY, PANAMA
Madame President's Secret Surf Spot

It's not every day you meet a nation's president. During the Crossing Project's tour of duty aboard the *Indies Trader* in Panama, our good friends Linda and Joey Lalo took amazing care of us. A major clan in this tiny nation, the Lalos also own Panama's biggest surf shop.

When I brought two-time world champ Tom Carroll on the boat, they arranged for us to meet Mireya Moscoso, Panama's first female president, who was in office at the time. A petite, attractive, warm woman, she'd come from a poor family that lived in a relatively remote area on the coast. We had lunch with her, got a royal tour of the presidential palace, and then went into her office, where she took out a map and had us gather around.

It turned out as a kid she lived right on the shore and was a keen observer of the waves. She marked surf spots that still weren't accessible by car but could easily be reached by the *Indies Trader*. One, she said, had waves *"excepcionales."* We left with the map and soon followed her tip. She was, as Tom Carroll later observed, "right on the mark."

Grilled Asparagus with Crab Chipotle Mayonnaise

Our simple lunch was an elegant presentation of first-rate Panamanian cuisine. The Lalo family operates the biggest and best surf shop in Panama. They are dear friends and one of the finest families there or anywhere else. Matriarch Linda Lalo and her friend Mattie (who arranged our presidential visit) helped provide this recipe.

SERVES 6

24 thin asparagus spears, trimmed (about 1 pound)
2 tablespoons fresh lime juice, divided
¼ cup extra-virgin olive oil
¼ cup mayonnaise (light is fine)
¼ cup plain nonfat yogurt
¼ cup thinly sliced green onions, green parts only

2 celery stalks, diced
2 tablespoons adobo sauce (from a can of chipotles in adobo)
Sea salt and freshly ground pepper, to taste
2 cups fresh lump crabmeat, picked through for shells (about 1 pound)
2 tablespoons finely diced red onion
½ cup shaved Manchego cheese (about 2 ounces)

Fill a large skillet halfway with water and bring to a boil. Add asparagus and blanch until firm-tender, about 4 minutes. Drain, dunk in ice water until cool, and pat dry.

In a large serving bowl, combine asparagus, 1 tablespoon lime juice, and olive oil. In another bowl, mix mayonnaise, yogurt, green onions, celery, adobo sauce, and remaining lime juice.

Light a charcoal grill and bring to medium-low heat or preheat a gas grill to 325°F. Place spears on grill perpendicular to grate so they don't fall through. Grill for 1 minute, then turn and grill for 1 minute on other side. Repeat grill process once more, or until spears are grilled. Transfer asparagus to platter and season to taste with salt and pepper.

Add crab and red onion to adobo mixture and combine well. Spoon crab over asparagus, sprinkle with shaved Manchego, and serve directly from platter or divide equally among plates.

MOROCCO
Color, Clamor & Couscous

The Green Pentangle

Morocco is a mosaic of rococo color. The five-point black-bordered green star on the Moroccan flag represents the seal of Solomon, the color of hope, love, joy, wisdom, and peace. The red field it sits on is the color of Islam, but since Morocco's founding as a state more than a thousand years ago, it has been ruled by a series of independent dynasties. Now Africa's fifth-largest economy, it's a constitutional monarchy struggling against any form of domination.

The *Indies Trader* spent a month sailing the Moroccan coast before crossing the Atlantic to Brazil. Stretching from the straits of Gibraltar to the western Sahara, the 1,200 miles of shoreline offer waves and a cornucopia of cuisine. The coastal ranges in the east funnel offshore winter winds. Farmlands roll along the coastal plain, showing as frequent dots of green on a blanket of brown. The Moroccan seaboard arcs around North Africa, studded with dozens of points, bays, and beach breaks. Like zellige tilework, the clusters of seaside towns form geometric patterns rich with color and beauty. There are villages of oyster bays and Moorish castles, and ancient Phoenician seaports fronting the raw power of Atlantic surf. They meld to form a strange and wonderful Berber, French art deco, Moroccan exoticism.

The fish are in the boat.

The village of Taghazout, on Morocco's southern coast

Killer Seven-Vegetable Tagine 111

Marrakesh Butternut Squash Soup 112

Salad Taghazout 115

Shrimp Phyllo Purses with Tomato Chermoula Sauce 116

Agadir Almond Crunch 119

Moroccan Mint Tea 120

Moroccan Grilled Lamb Chops with Apricots & Prunes 123

Merguez Sausage 124

Harissa Sauce 125

Baked Fish with Almond Sauce 126

Couscous Casablanca 129

ANCHOR POINT, TAGHAZOUT

Anchor Point Azure

One late October, during my second sojourn to Europe, Jim Ahern invited me to come to a then-almost-unknown village on Morocco's southern coast where he'd surfed a powerful point with the ominous name Killers. Ahern had been a seminal character at my school, where he'd taught a number of us how to shape hot surfboards, drive cool cars, and for some, speak clearly while dangling a lit cigarette from your bottom lip.

Ahern showed me grainy footage of the surf. Scary as it looked, I couldn't resist. I'd never seen an ocean that color of bright azure. An old Berber campsite, Anchor Point had been discovered by surfers only a few years before, and already it had a reputation as a world-class wave.

It was a four-day drive down National Route 1, a journey not unlike the one on Pacific Coast Highway in Northern California, but without the greenery. Along the route were little roadside stands serving steaming falafels, sweet dates, and fresh, spicy salads. We arrived on an evening just after sundown. The low, camel-scented desert wind lifted the white crests of the swells just enough to catch the fading light. The waves were double overhead and broke 300 yards down the point in a straight, feathering line. That year the surf remained big but rideable almost every day through late December.

Tents were all we could afford. We ate a lot of couscous with vegetable tagines.

Killer Seven-Vegetable Tagine

Tagines are both recipes and the pots they're cooked in, with wide, shallow bottoms and tall, conical tops. A Dutch oven is a good substitute for a tagine, but use the real thing if you can get one. This tagine dish is one of the succulent, savory, slow-cooked stews Morocco is famous for.

I like to quickly stir-fry the vegetables before stewing them to seal in flavor and a bit of char. This sear-then-wet-cooking method retains the vegetables' nutrient-rich, flavor-intensified juices. Moroccans use the seven-vegetable combo for good luck. This simple recipe will bring good health, too.

Note: Use Tunisian extra-virgin olive oil (available at Trader Joe's) for North African authenticity.

SERVES 6, with leftovers

1 cup sliced carrots (1-inch rounds)
1 cup sliced zucchini (1-inch rounds)
1 cup sliced yellow summer squash
  (1-inch rounds)
1 cup sliced onions (½ inch thick)
1 cup red bell pepper (1-inch pieces)
1 cup green beans (1-inch-long pieces)
1 cup Japanese eggplant (1-inch pieces)
1 sweet hot cherry pepper, minced (or 1
  teaspoon red pepper flakes)

1½ teaspoons ground cumin
1 teaspoon sweet paprika
½ teaspoon ground ginger
½ teaspoon ground turmeric
Pinch of cayenne pepper
¼ cup extra-virgin olive oil
1 cup chicken or vegetable broth
Sea salt and freshly ground black
  pepper, to taste

Mix vegetables and spices in a mixing bowl.

In a large tagine or Dutch oven, heat oil to almost smoking. Toss vegetables into pan and sear, stir-frying for 2 minutes or so. Add broth and cook over high heat until liquid is absorbed, about 5 minutes, adding salt and pepper to taste. Remove from heat, cover, and let flavors combine for about 15 minutes.

Serve with couscous and lamb as part of a Moroccan meal, or with anything you'd like.

Will Play for Veggies

My friend Jake Shimabukuro is a Hawaiian virtuoso who has reinvented the technique of playing ukulele. Check YouTube for his four-string version of "While My Guitar Gently Weeps" and you'll become an instant believer. A few years ago, Jake performed to help me raise money for the California Surf Museum, and the band needed to eat. He's a vegetarian, so I cooked a Moroccan vegetable tagine for his whole entourage, and it was a big hit.

JEMAA EL-FNA, MARRAKESH
Midnight Marrakesh Express

The train from Tangier to Marrakesh in Crosby, Stills, and Nash's hit single is not just a lyric—it's a cultural experience.

In the early surf days, Morocco was best traversed by train. They were fast and cheap, but sleeping on the overnight cars on hard wooden bench seats was tough. On one early trip I discovered a covert comfort zone: the baggage coach. I stacked my backpack and surfboard behind piles of baggage, climbed over a wire cage barrier, and sank into the malleable mail sacks, becoming invisible. I fell asleep to the drone of Isha, the late evening prayer, mixed with the rhythm of the steel rails.

In the middle of the night, the train lurched to a stop at a desolate railway station. A troop of soldiers boarded, boots banging on the floor. I heard coach door after coach door open and slam shut, the soldiers' shouting interspersed with a few shrieks from startled women woken by the din. The soldiers burst into the baggage compartment, and for a moment I thought they were going to see me. When I breathed again, they were gone, and they found their prey moments later. As the train started up again, I saw from the slit window the shackled suspect on his knees, the soldiers surrounding him like jackals with a baby goat. I didn't sleep anymore that night.

Morning brought us into the old Marrakesh station. By that afternoon we were surfing the long, rocky wave at Anchor Point. The first food I ate there was a butternut squash soup, and after twenty hours on a train, nothing had ever tasted so good.

Marrakesh Butternut Squash Soup

In nomadic tribes, personal items become multi-purpose. And a single word can become an entire cultural connection, since there is far less compartmentalizing in Bedouin society. To Tuareg Berbers, *guedra* means cauldron/cooking pot. But it is often covered with an animal skin, creating a drum that's also called a guedra. The drum is used to play a heartbeat rhythm (life's basic cadence) that is called a guedra as well. And female dancers—also called guedras—perform a joyful,

celebrative, trance-like dance that (once again) is called a guedra. So depending on its context, one word can mean cooking pot, drum, life rhythm, dancer, or ritual ceremony.

Blue people consider guedra their direct contact with the elements, spirits, and universe—the deepest expression of their souls and protection against a hostile environment and evil spirits. All I know is if you cook this simple, colorful, lip-smacking soup, everyone you share it with will experience a surf-stoked trance dance in their mouth.

SERVES 6

1 head garlic, roasted
2 tablespoons coconut oil (or any cooking oil)
1 red bell pepper, chopped
1 sweet onion, chopped
1 large butternut squash, peeled and cut into
  1-inch cubes (about 4 cups)
1 teaspoon *ras el hanout* spice mix, preferably
  Spicely brand
1 teaspoon smoked paprika
½ teaspoon cumin
½ teaspoon cinnamon

½ teaspoon cayenne pepper
½ teaspoon chopped fresh thyme
  (or ¼ teaspoon dried)
2 cups cold canned coconut milk, divided
2 cups vegetable broth
2 tablespoons minced fresh ginger, divided
4 ounces goat cheese, crumbled, divided
½ cup chopped fresh cilantro
24 to 30 pistachios, chopped
30 to 36 pomegranate seeds

Remove roasted garlic cloves from their skins, mash with a fork, and set aside.

Heat coconut oil in a large soup pot. Add red bell pepper and onion, and cook until soft, 3 to 5 minutes. Add squash, *ras el hanout*, smoked paprika, cumin, cinnamon, cayenne, and thyme. Cook for 3 to 5 minutes, then pour in 1½ cups coconut milk, vegetable broth, and 1 tablespoon minced ginger. Bring soup to a boil, cover, reduce heat to low, and simmer until squash is tender, 20 to 25 minutes.

While soup is cooking, make the ginger cream. Combine remaining ½ cup coconut milk and 1 tablespoon ginger in a small bowl and set aside.

Once butternut squash is tender, mix in mashed garlic and half the crumbled goat cheese. Remove pot from heat and purée soup in a blender or food processor until smooth. Return soup to pot on stove and reheat gently.

To serve, ladle soup into 6 bowls. Drizzle coconut ginger cream over soup and swirl with a spoon. Top each serving with equal portions of cilantro, pistachios, and remaining crumbled goat cheese. Garnish with pomegranate seeds and serve.

TAMNI, NEAR AGADIR
Yellow Horned Vipers & Flying Goats

The view along Morocco's N1 route from Essaouira to Agadir is lined with pounding surf, deranged drivers, yellow horned vipers, and flying goats. You don't want to get hit by any of them. But sighting goats perched ten, fifteen, twenty feet up in a tree is as startling as swerving to miss a vegetable truck or setting your surfboard down next to a coiled viper. Well, maybe not quite, but it's certainly more bizarre.

These bright white tree-climbing goats are unique to the Agadir region. So are the thorny argan trees—and they are the only kind the goats climb, because they're apparently addicted to the bulbous fruit. I've seen as many as ten in *one tree*. Once balanced on the branches, the goats gobble the fruit, digest the pulp, eject the softened seeds, and move on to the next tree. These seeds are collected from the droppings by diligent Moroccan women, then cracked and mashed to produce the precious argan oil.

The area surrounding Essaouira is a center of the country's highly lucrative argan oil production, a prized ingredient in cosmetics. Although most argan oil comes from seeds harvested by farmers picking the fruit, the goat method is still in regular use.

As Julia Roberts' character said in *Notting Hill,* "Happiness isn't happiness without a violin-playing goat." Or a flying one, I guess.

How many goats can you count in the tree?

Salad Taghazout
Olives, Walnuts, Oranges, Goat Cheese & Baby Lettuces

Moroccans serve salads like this over rice, and it's delicious. So feel free to do the same.

SERVES 4

1 Valencia orange

1 head butter or Bibb lettuce

1 cup shredded white cabbage

2 tablespoons extra-virgin olive oil

1 tablespoon fresh lemon juice

2 tablespoons chopped fresh dill

½ teaspoon ground cumin

½ teaspoon sweet paprika

¾ cup chopped walnuts

½ cup pitted Kalamata olives

1 ounce soft goat cheese, separated
   into small chunks

4 parsley sprigs

4 dill sprigs

Peel orange and divide into sections. Keep chilled in fridge until ready to use.

Wash and dry lettuce, then gently tear leaves into bite-size pieces and combine in salad bowl with cabbage.

In a small bowl, stir olive oil, lemon juice, dill, cumin, and paprika together, mixing well to combine. Fold in walnuts, olives, goat cheese, and orange sections, until all ingredients are coated in dressing. Pour over lettuce and toss.

Serve from bowl or on individual salad plates, garnishing each with a sprig of parsley and dill.

Shrimp Phyllo Purses with Tomato Chermoula Sauce

I know, "phyllo purses" sounds challenging and complicated, but this dish is easier than it sounds. Just wrap up your ingredients in a little sack, bake them in the oven, and you have a dish that's both impressive and delicious.

SERVES 6

2 tablespoons extra-virgin olive oil

2 cups chopped green onions

2 cloves garlic, minced

1½ teaspoons ground cumin

1 teaspoon sweet paprika

18 large shrimp, peeled, deveined, and coarsely chopped (about 12 ounces)

4 ounces cooked bean threads or superfine rice noodles, minced

⅓ cup chopped fresh parsley

¼ cup chopped fresh cilantro

3 tablespoons fresh lemon juice

9 sheets frozen phyllo pastry, defrosted

½ cup unsalted butter (1 stick), melted

6 teaspoons panko breadcrumbs

6 fresh chives

Tomato Chermoula Sauce (*recipe follows*)

Heat oil in large skillet over medium heat. Add green onions, garlic, cumin, and paprika. Sauté until onions turn golden, about 3 minutes. Add shrimp and sauté until cooked through, about 3 minutes. Remove from heat and stir in minced bean threads, parsley, cilantro, and lemon juice. Set aside.

Preheat oven to 400°F. Using an 8-inch-diameter plate as a guide, cut phyllo sheets into 18 8-inch rounds. Cover rounds with damp paper towel.

Place 1 phyllo round on work surface and brush with melted butter. Top with second phyllo round; brush with melted butter. Top with third phyllo round; brush with melted butter. Sprinkle with 1 teaspoon breadcrumbs, and place one-sixth of shrimp filling in center of phyllo. Close filling by gathering phyllo and carefully twisting top to form a purse.

Transfer phyllo purse to baking sheet. Repeat with remaining phyllo rounds, melted butter, breadcrumbs, and filling, forming 6 phyllo purses total. Brush phyllo purses with butter.

Bake phyllo purses until outside is golden and filling is heated through, about 12 minutes. Carefully tie 1 chive around twisted section of each phyllo purse, forming a knot. Transfer 1 phyllo purse to each of 6 plates. Spoon some Tomato Chermoula Sauce around each phyllo purse and serve.

TOMATO CHERMOULA SAUCE

2 tablespoons extra-virgin olive oil

1 clove garlic, minced

1 teaspoon ground cumin

1 teaspoon sweet paprika

1¾ pounds tomatoes, seeded, chopped,
  and roasted (about 3 cups)

¼ cup chopped fresh cilantro

¼ cup chopped fresh parsley

Heat oil in medium saucepan over medium heat. Add garlic, cumin, and paprika, and sauté about 2 minutes. Add roasted tomatoes, cilantro, and parsley. Cook, stirring occasionally, for about 8 minutes. Set aside until needed; you can store this sauce in the refrigerator for a few days.

SILVER SOUK, ESSAOUIRA
Silver Souks

Souks (marketplaces) are the beating heart of North African life. Essaouira's souk is known for its silver; necklaces, earrings, inlaid daggers, ornate teapots, and filigreed trays are just the shiny tip of the market's iceberg of activity. But for me, the most overpowering attraction of the labyrinth-like jumble of stalls is the food.

Teasha and Joe Curren traveled and surfed in Morocco, and she wrote this in an article called "Pirates, Belching Camels, and Right-Hand Peelers":

"A wood-fired oven bakes crusty baguettes delivered by bicycle throughout the neighborhood. Above the fish market hundreds of seagulls swirl around the watchtower waiting to swoop on the morsels left from the daily catch. Competitive chefs create elaborate displays of food, artistically arranged to lure the hungry: salads, couscous, fried fish, kebabs, fruit, vegetables, mountains of flatbread; sheep's head soup and massive bowls of steaming snails. Herb-infused aromas of tagines escape from clay pots simmering over charcoal fires. Freshly plucked chickens, the hindquarters of a cow, and the tailed carcass of a goat dangle on large hooks. Clusters of women carry bags filled with purchases, stirring up gauzy dust, veils turning silver in the falling light."

A Marrakesh souk: Like shiny fishbones, the maze of streets splays outward.

Agadir Almond Crunch

MAKES 24 SMALL PIECES

¼ teaspoon ground saffron

2 tablespoons rose water

1 cup sugar

3 tablespoons honey

¼ cup corn oil or other neutral-flavored oil

1½ cups unsalted slivered blanched almonds

¼ cup unsalted pistachios, chopped

Spread a piece of parchment paper on a baking sheet. In a small bowl, dissolve ground saffron in rose water, and set aside.

Melt sugar, honey, and oil together in a heavy saucepan over medium heat for 5 minutes, stirring occasionally. Add slivered almonds to mixture, and continue stirring for 2 to 3 minutes, until mixture turns a golden color and starts to coagulate. Add saffron-rosewater mixture to syrup and cook for another 2 to 4 minutes. Stir occasionally with a wooden spoon until mixture turns a golden brown color. To determine doneness, you can drop a small spoonful of hot almond mixture into a bowl of ice water. If it hardens immediately, candy is ready. Reduce heat to a simmer.

Place heaping spoonfuls of mixture on parchment paper at 1-inch intervals. Sprinkle pistachios onto mounds and make sure they stick in hot mixture. Let candy cool thoroughly, then remove from parchment and store in an airtight container.

Moroccan Mint Tea

MAKES 4 CUPS

5 teaspoons gunpowder green tea leaves,
  or any green tea
5 cups boiling water

Sugar or other sweetener, to taste
Mint sprigs

Put green tea in teapot and pour in 1 cup boiling water. Swirl to warm pot and rinse tea.
Strain out and discard water, reserving tea leaves in pot. Pour remaining 4 cups boiling water into
teapot and let steep 2 minutes. Add sweetener and mint sprigs to taste, and steep 3 to 4 minutes
more before serving.

ESSAOUIRA BAY, ESSAOUIRA
Purple Islands & Castles Made of Sand

The ocean-facing parapets of Essaouira's walled fortress look across a fleet of small skiffs protected by a narrow harbor. A broad, sandy beach extends from the harbor south along a moon-shaped bay, slightly sheltered from the surf by the Iles Purpuraires. Phoenician navigators reached these "purple islands" in the fifth century, lured by the murex mollusks covering the shorelines. The crushed shells produce a dye ranging between indigo, royal blue, and lilac, a color we call Phoenician purple today, after the traders who first harvested them.

The whitewashed walls and lavender shutters turn a violet hue in morning sunlight, and in *Game of Thrones's* third season, the directors turned this ancient seaport into a film set for Slaver's Bay.

Along the waterfront, small cafés serve Moroccan mint tea and black coffee. On that strand I wrote stories, rode waves, drank mint tea with brown sugar, and listened to *Axis Bold as Love* on an eight-track tape player in my 1967 Volkswagen camper bus. The sand there was buttery, and the camels sometimes walked along the beach, in front of the waves that broke at odd intervals—consistent and punchy, like the reggae master Bob Marley, who purportedly visited here. The Canary Current pulls southward, enhancing the fishing industry and amplifying the long, corrugated swell lines that sweep down from the North Atlantic. They break in a field of peaks cracking like the rusty cannons on the ramparts facing out to sea.

Despite the story that Jimi Hendrix's song "Castles Made of Sand" was inspired by his visit to the mauve sandstone-colored castles of Essaouira, he actually wrote it two years before he visited here. But in the narrow alleys of the medieval medina, long slivers of sun still light up the brightly painted doorways, and the tall minarets still silhouette against the purple haze that kisses this sky.

Even the boats cast a purple hue.

Moroccan Grilled Lamb Chops with Apricots & Prunes

One of the best recipes I discovered in Morocco was the amazing mix of fruit and meat.
Serve it with couscous with chopped mint, toasted slivered almonds, and grated lemon peel.
Add an Australian Shiraz or full-bodied Syrah from the Languedoc, and you've got a special dinner.

SERVES 6

12 small lamb chops, cut 1½ inches thick
   (about 3 pounds)
¼ cup extra-virgin olive oil
2 cups white wine, divided
1 large onion, finely chopped
8 cloves garlic, minced
2 cups low-salt chicken broth
2 teaspoons red pepper flakes
1½ teaspoons ground cumin
1½ teaspoons salt
1 teaspoon *ras el hanout* spice mix, preferably
   Spicely brand
1 teaspoon ground coriander

½ teaspoon cayenne pepper
½ teaspoon freshly ground black pepper
2 tablespoons extra-virgin olive oil
1 tablespoon minced fresh ginger
1 tablespoon tomato paste
2 teaspoons (packed) grated lemon peel
1 cup prunes in jar with juice, pitted
1 tablespoon cornstarch
2 tablespoons water
8 fresh ripe yellow apricots, pitted and quartered
3 large firm plum tomatoes, quartered
2 tablespoons chopped fresh cilantro

Marinate lamb chops in mixture of olive oil and ½ cup wine for a minimum of 1 hour, or overnight.
In large pot or casserole dish, sauté onion over medium-high heat until soft, about 5 minutes. Add
garlic and sauté for 1 minute more.

Add broth and remaining wine and reduce heat to medium. Mix in all spices, olive oil, ginger,
tomato paste, and lemon peel, and bring to a boil. Add sautéed onion-garlic mixture and juice from
prune jar (about ½ cup). Reduce heat and cook on low for 1 hour, stirring occasionally.

Meanwhile, light a charcoal grill and bring to medium-high heat or preheat a gas grill to 350°F to
400°F. Place marinated lamb on grill and cook until browned on all sides, turning once. Cook until well-
charred but very rare inside. When done, transfer lamb and drippings to broth pot and simmer uncovered
until lamb is just tender, about 40 minutes. Transfer lamb to platter, tent loosely with foil, and let rest.

Mix cornstarch and water vigorously and drizzle into pot. Continue cooking sauce until thick
enough to coat spoon, about 20 minutes. Fold in prunes, apricots, and tomatoes and heat until fruit is
just soft, about 5 minutes. Pour over lamb, sprinkle with cilantro, and serve.

*The Tuareg Berbers are often referred to as "the Blue Men of the desert," because their
robes are dyed blue. These nomads pounding indigo stones into powder and then pound the
powder into the fabric. Their camel-caravans still appear unexpectedly, sweeping over the
horizon and into the Saharan village of Goulimine before melting into the desert again.*

CAMEL CARAVAN, GOULIMINE
Goulimine Gold

In the early summer one year, my friend and street tutor Jim Ahern invited me to the distant town of Goulimine, where camel caravans plodded past date palms through the gates of the red-clay-walled city from the dusty plains of the western Sahara. On the road into town, the camels move slowly, in rhythm, belching and drooling in the dry heat, their backs piled with goods. Tribes come from as far away as Niger, and the camels carry their goods to sell. Each tribe had different colors of dress, and when they camped, the wind carried the smell of lamb sizzling on makeshift grills.

Ahern was there to find Goulimine beads, much in demand in the Paris flea market. In past centuries these kaleidoscopic glass beads, actually Venetian in origin, were used as trading currency. In that early surf era they were a new-age fashion craze, like puka shells in Hawaii, Balinese batiks, and abalone shells from Baja. The markup was twenty-fold, and the business (unlike the hashish trade) was safe, legal, and fun. These exotic beads were worth their weight in gold. Jim brought back a carload and lived on the profits for months.

MARRAKESH

Red City Surgery

Marrakesh is called the Red City because of the color of its walls and buildings, but the shade is closer to a dirty orange brick. When there are festivals, the Red City buzzes like a beehive and celebrants light up the narrow streets. One November evening on an early trip with Jim Ahern, we watched from a sidewalk café as a parade swept across the square and down the wide street toward the old mosque with a tall minaret. In the middle of the mass of revelers were acrobats and scorpion eaters with masks and embroidered costumes. Musicians marched by, playing screeching flutes and clashing cymbals in rhythm with the drums as guedra dancers in bright blue cloaks leaped and contorted in long ripples of color. Clusters of young teen boys swaying from halting carts brought up the rear of the procession, singing and chanting in their silk robes and bright caps, surrounded by older women.

Ahern turned and said, "These poor little guys are going to the circumcision ceremony. Hot knives. Like lambs to slaughter. They all get done at the same time."

Merguez Sausage

Merguez is a spicy red sausage made with ground lamb and lots of red chiles, paprika, herbs, and harissa sauce. It makes a great hors d'oeuvre or a main meal served with vegetables or couscous. And it fits the theme of the Red City. I first had this dish in Safi, a town that Tom Carroll told me has one of the best point waves in Morocco—it's a fickle wave that only breaks on a big swell. Twenty years ago, we didn't even know it was there.

SERVES 6 AS AN APPETIZER

1 pound ground lamb
½ cup Harissa Sauce (*recipe follows*)
3 cloves garlic, roasted and chopped

2 tablespoons chopped fresh cilantro
2 tablespoons merguez spice mix
Sausage casings (optional)

Combine all ingredients except sausage casings (if using) in a large bowl, kneading the mixture well to evenly distribute spices, herbs, and harissa sauce. Shape into 5 x 1-inch cigars, or shape as desired.

Alternatively, you can pass the ingredients through a meat grinder and feed the merguez mixture into sausage casings.

For best flavor, allow merguez to sit for 30 minutes (or longer in fridge) before cooking. Brush sausages with oil and grill or broil them until browned and cooked through. Or you can fry them in a little oil until well browned all over.

Serve over chopped and steamed cauliflower with additional harissa sauce.

Harissa Sauce

1 red bell pepper
½ teaspoon coriander seeds
½ teaspoon cumin seeds
½ teaspoon caraway seeds
1½ tablespoons extra-virgin olive oil
1 small red onion, coarsely chopped

3 cloves garlic, coarsely chopped
3 hot red chiles, seeded and chopped
2 tablespoons fresh lemon juice
1½ teaspoons tomato paste
Sea salt, to taste

Roast red bell pepper over a gas flame or under a very hot broiler until blackened on outside and completely soft (about 25 minutes). Transfer to a bowl, cover with plastic wrap, and let cool. Once cool, peel pepper and discard its skin and seeds.

Lightly toast coriander, cumin, and caraway seeds for about 2 minutes in a dry skillet over medium-low heat, then set aside.

Heat olive oil in a skillet over medium heat. Sauté onion, garlic, and chiles until almost caramelized, then add lemon juice and tomato paste.

Put all ingredients in a blender and process until smooth, adding a little oil if needed. Season with salt to taste, and store in a container in the fridge for up to 2 weeks.

DAR BOUAZZA, CASABLANCA
White City, Whitefish, Whitecaps

The port of Casablanca is famous for its seafood. Port de Pêche in the center of the fishing harbor is one of the best seafood restaurants in town. Whitewashed walls are warm but faded, and the place still has a hint of art deco brought by the French during their half-century colonial takeover of the western Sahara. Always packed at noon and sundown, Port de Pêche serves twenty kinds of seafood prepared ten different ways.

You can walk farther, deep into the heart of the harbor—just follow your nose as the briny smell gets stronger. You'll find little temporary bars with wooden benches where you can eat cheaply, or you can go behind the lighthouse along the ruins of some old buildings and join the locals for a barbecue on the rocky beachfront.

Casablanca is not a great surf spot, but the beaches are beauties, and the winding alleyways invoke the ghosts of Bogart and the famous film's café. If some parts of the city's architecture have been worn like an old Bedouin fabric, others have been preserved by proud Moroccan families. And there are plenty of quality waves just down the road.

Baked Fish with Almond Sauce

This dish comes from the fishing village of Safi, which has one of the best waves in Morocco. It is a recipe adapted from *Couscous and Other Good Food from Morocco* by Paula Wolfert, who's considered an authority on Moroccan cuisine. I've made it many times and it never fails to satisfy. Serve with salad, couscous, and Killer Seven-Vegetable Tagine (*see page 111*).

SERVES 6

1½ cups chopped almonds
1½ cups powdered sugar
⅓ cup water
¼ cup vegetable or canola oil
6 tablespoons unsalted butter (¾ stick), softened and divided

1 tablespoon orange flower water (available in most markets)
1 teaspoon ground cinnamon
2 cups minced onions
6 striped sea bass fillets

In a small skillet over medium-low heat, toast almonds, stirring continuously until golden. Transfer to paper towels to cool. Once cooled, place almonds, sugar, water, oil, 3 tablespoons butter, orange flower water, and cinnamon into a blender, and pulverize into a smooth paste.

Preheat oven to 375°F. Grease a large baking dish with butter, then spoon minced onions into dish with a little water to form a bed for fish. Place fish fillets over onion bed, and use a spatula to spread almond paste over fish. Melt remaining butter and drizzle over fish.

Roast until fish is cooked through and paste is just crusty and beginning to fall into onion sauce, about 35 minutes.

CHEFCHAOUEN, RIF MOUNTAINS
Moroccan Blond

Cannabis has been cultivated in the Rif region and beyond since the seventh century. Cultivation and transformation of cannabis is a $2 billion industry, representing more than six percent of Morocco's GDP. Nearly eighty percent of the cannabis resin (hashish) consumed in Europe comes from this mostly mountainous terrain in northern Morocco. And for good reason: Moroccan Blond is a fine, compressed hash oil of high quality that is said to provide a light, energetic high.

Moroccan blond has another meaning, describing the people defined by lighter skin and fairer hair than most other Berbers. These are mostly Rifians, an ethnic group that looks quite different from the predominant North African tribal peoples. Many of their ancestors were Europeans, some of whom were brought to North Africa as slaves.

Like all Moroccans, Moroccan blonds love the spicy harissa that adds heat and a complex flavor to any dish.

Rory Russell, a true "Moroccan blond," en route to Anchor Point in the late '70s

Couscous Casablanca

Moroccans use a two-part vessel called a couscoussière to make couscous. It consists of a flat-based colander (a *keskes*) that sits snugly atop a deep pot called a *bourma*. The pot holds the simmering broth and vegetables while the couscous steams in the colander above. If you don't have a couscoussière, a stockpot and a colander with holes on the bottom only (not the sides) will work. Authentic couscous requires several steamings, but I've never seen the flavor payoff for all the work involved.

Couscous doesn't have much flavor, but it's light and absorbs other flavors beautifully, so traditionally it's served with seasonal vegetables and a rich broth. I pair it with Killer Seven-Vegetable Tagine (*see page 111*); the tagine's broth is perfect as the steaming liquid for couscous.

Add a fresh grilled fish, pour a little Harissa Sauce over it, and you have a complete and delicious meal.

SERVES 6

1 tablespoon unsalted butter

1 large onion, halved and cut in 1/4-inch-thick slices (about 1 cup)

1 clove garlic, crushed

2 cups couscous

½ cup minced cilantro or parsley

Sea salt and freshly ground pepper, to taste

½ cup golden raisins

1 tablespoon Harissa Sauce, homemade (*see page 125*) or Spicely brand (optional)

Heat butter over medium heat in large saucepan. Add sliced onions, stir, and cook until soft and starting to caramelize, 15 to 20 minutes, stirring occasionally and lowering the heat if they start to burn. Stir in crushed garlic, and cook 1 minute more.

While you're making the Killer Seven-Vegetable Tagine, place couscous in colander above cooking vegetables and steam for 10 minutes. Remove from heat, cover, and let stand for 5 minutes. Stir in cilantro or parsley. Add salt and pepper to taste.

Arrange caramelized onions and ½ cup raisins in a ring around couscous on the serving platter. Serve with Harissa Sauce (if you like it), and pair with the vegetable tagine.

HAWAII
Birthplace of Surfing, Axis of Fusion Food

As the editor of *Surfer,* I was able to cover Hawaii's North Shore winter season—and it was the high point of the year. I'd rent a house for several months, and our team of writers and photographers would shoot photos, conduct interviews, and cover the stories chronicling the world's best surfers in the world's best waves. Not bad work if you can get it.

Considered the birthplace of surfing, the Hawaiian Islands are the ultimate testing ground for surfers from around the globe. Most of the innovation in surfboards and maneuvers was either conceived or proved in the Islands. For four months of winter, it is the focus of the surf world.

For both local and visiting surfers, eating is the second most popular pursuit after wave riding. Influenced by the many cultures that have migrated to Hawaii over the last three centuries, the Islands have led the new wave of fusion cooking. Mixing and matching Polynesian dishes with contributions from China, Korea, Portugal, Japan, the Philippines, and the mainland US, Hawaiian cuisine is one of the most diverse and delicious in the world. When you add in the quality of the local produce, seafood, and meat, you have a knockout culinary destination.

North Shore Oahu colors come in as many varieties as the waves.

Macadamia-Crusted Mahi Mahi 133

Café Haleiwa Banana Pancakes 137

Bethany Hamilton's Smoothies 138

Rell Sunn's Kalua Turkey 143

Ono Poke Bowl 145

Salad Bar 147

Porterhouse Steak with Herbed Butter & Portuguese Chimichurri 148

The "Maitai" Mai Tai 151

Korean Short Ribs 152

PAIA, MAUI
Pleasant Mountain

In the autumn of my junior year, I attended Mauna'olu College, up the slope of Haleakala Crater, surrounded by pineapple fields and overlooking the islands of Kahoolawe, Lanai, and Molokai. No longer operating, Mauna'olu—"pleasant mountain" in Hawaiian—was founded in 1861 as a seminary school for women, and it was a fine campus. In the plantation-style great house were two stories of lanais, floor-to-ceiling windows, and more than thirty rooms. We took classes in drawing rooms and ate meals in the huge dining hall. Below the rolling, grassy grounds, a cluster of cane houses served as our dorms.

The 200-yard walk down the hill to the dorms could be shortcut by a seventy-yard tiptoe across an irrigation aqueduct spanning a deep ravine. After dinner, we'd drink and smoke on the lawn in the darkness before traversing the six-inch-wide ledges. The drop was more than three stories to rocky red dirt. No one ever fell. But I still think of that ledge sometimes on dark nights.

Tropical Maui was a good place to complete my science classes: oceanography, marine biology, and aquarium science. Those classes introduced me to the surf break at Maalaea Harbor, where we once scored amazing waves but mostly counted the movements of pipipi snails along the breakwater for our biology class. The combination of surf checking and data research was a lot like waiting for a blue moon and watching magic mushrooms sprout. Ho'okipa was our messy but reliable surf spot. Today Ho'okipa is world renowned for windsurfing and gourmet food trucks, but back then it was the domain of beachside fishermen, a handful of surfers, and giant green turtles that occasionally attracted sharks.

Macadamia-Crusted Mahi Mahi

East on the road that leads to Hana is the tiny village of Kuau, where a restaurant named Wooden Ships opened right on the beach. Cheap yet gourmet, it didn't last long—but I still have the poster of the place. For a long time now, it's been home to the acclaimed Mama's Fish House. It's worth a trip to the east side just for Mama's mahi mahi.

SERVES 6

6 mahi mahi fillets (1 inch thick—about 5 ounces each)

Sea salt, to taste (preferably Alaea red Hawaiian sea salt)

Freshly ground pepper

¾ cup herbed panko breadcrumbs

¾ cup finely chopped coconut-glazed macadamia nuts

1½ cups all-purpose flour

2 large eggs mixed with ¼ cup milk

⅓ cup extra-light olive oil, or other neutral oil for cooking

2 jiggers brandy

¼ cup heavy cream

4 tablespoons (½ stick) butter

2 tablespoons slivered fresh garlic

3 blood oranges, peeled and separated into segments, or use berries, roasted peppers, or other garnishes

1 tablespoon freshly chopped basil

1 tablespoon freshly chopped parsley

6 lemon wedges

Season fillets lightly with sea salt and cracked pepper. Mix panko and chopped macadamia nuts together in a small bowl. Dust fish fillets with flour, dip in egg mixture, then coat with panko mixture, pressing to adhere.

Heat a large sauté pan over medium heat and coat with oil. When oil is hot, add fish and sauté on one side for about 2 minutes. Adjust cooking time if your fillets are thinner or thicker than 1 inch. Do not let nut crust burn. Turn over and cook other side until fish is just done. Be careful to not overcook fish.

Remove fish from pan and set on serving plates. Deglaze pan with brandy, cream, and butter. Stir mixture and simmer gently until brandy evaporates and liquid becomes a thickened sauce. Add garlic and sauté for another minute, or until garlic becomes fragrant. Spoon sauce over fish. Place 3 or 4 blood orange segments or other garnishes on top of each fillet. Sprinkle basil and parsley over fillets. Squeeze a wedge of lemon juice on each fillet. Serve immediately.

PUNALAU, MAUI
The Pig Farm at Punalau

One winter, I stayed with good friend Brent Schlea at the pig farm at Punalau, just up the road from the surf at Honolua Bay. The old cane house we lived in looked across the highway and pineapple fields to the distant outline of Molokai. The Molokai channel was a cobalt-colored stream, and the Aleutian swells threaded the stack of other islands that try to block their march.

The road wound past the cane house, turning to dirt as it reached the cliffs that washed out in winter rains. There were only two dwellings on the property and no electricity. We cooked on an open grill and rinsed in an outdoor shower. At twilight the air was still, and we could hear the neighbor's pigs above the sweet night voices of birds. The stench from the pigsties was strong, and when the Kona winds blew from upcountry, the kitchen had to be wiped clean and clothes had to be washed before you could wear them again.

We prayed for trade winds.

PAIA, MAUI
Wagashi & Movies

Not far away from Mauna'olu College, which I attended for a memorable semester, was Paia, a tattered little junction where Paia Fats ruled the corner pool hall and the circa-1910 cinema screened color-drenched Samurai sagas, the southeast shore's only evening entertainment. The lobby had curling chips of faded paint, and the short, wrinkled proprietress served Japanese *wagashi*—rice or bean sweets—like *daifuku, dango,* and *amanatto.* In the days of Maui Wowie, students and surfers alike found these rather savory sweets far more satisfying than popcorn.

It was less than a minute's walk to a view of the Punalau surf. So for us, living so close, it was easy to check it— ten times a day. Which, between us all, we did.

HALEIWA, OAHU
A Bonzer Breakfast

The most patronized breakfast spot on Oahu's north shore, Café Haleiwa is the pride of surfer Duncan Campbell and his family. With a gravel parking lot in back, a steaming open kitchen in the middle, and a homey front breakfast room, it's home to most of the local surfers at least one day a week.

Along with his brother Malcolm, Duncan developed the Bonzer, universally credited as the first modern tri-fin surfboard. In the years when the Campbell brothers brought their revolutionary design into *Surfer*, we championed the design, even as it struggled to gain the prominence that later multi-fin versions received.

Duncan's creative ingenuity transferred from the shaping bay to the kitchen the moment he opened Café Haleiwa. On any given morning, the surf stars are as thick as the flapjacks. For two decades, he's made this humble breakfast diner one of the surf world's most beloved establishments.

Duncan Campbell at Café Haleiwa

Café Haleiwa Banana Pancakes

I've never cared for thick, gooey pancakes—they taste like eating dough. My favorites are fluffy on the inside, crispy on the outside, infused with the delicate flavor of fresh fruit and vanilla. Just like these.

MAKES 12 4-INCH PANCAKES

1½ cups all-purpose flour

2 tablespoons sugar

2½ teaspoons baking powder

½ teaspoon salt

2 large eggs

1 cup lowfat milk, plus more if needed

½ teaspoon vanilla extract

2 jiggers brandy

1 small, overripe banana, peeled and mashed

½ cup fresh blueberries

3 tablespoons unsalted butter, melted,
  plus more for pan

Vegetable oil

¼ cup shredded coconut

½ cup pecans, broken in bits

In a medium mixing bowl, sift together flour, sugar, baking powder and salt. Whisk in eggs, then add 1 cup milk, vanilla, and brandy, and whisk until well blended.

Gently fold mashed banana and blueberries into flour mixture, then drizzle in melted butter. With a rubber spatula, mix batter gently until thin and smooth. Add a little more milk if batter is thick and lumpy.

Heat a griddle or nonstick pan over medium heat. Drizzle in a teaspoon of melted butter and a teaspoon of vegetable oil to coat the griddle. Pour or spoon onto pan, using about ¼ cup batter for each pancake. Leave room between pancakes. Flip pancakes when holes form on top and underside is golden brown, about 2 minutes. Cook until bottom is golden brown and top is puffed, 1 to 2 minutes more.

Using spatula, transfer pancakes to a serving plate. Wipe griddle clean with paper towels, then add more butter and oil. Repeat process with remaining batter.

Sprinkle each pancake with shredded coconut and pecan bits. Serve with maple syrup and sliced bananas.

HANALEI BAY, KAUAI
Just Bethany's Dad

During my college days, I had a couple of surf chums, Peter and Tom, who would shoot down to Baja with me in my '69 Volkswagen camper van. Both were super-solid surfers and stand-up guys—generous, humble, and fearless. We'd surf and camp and cook on my little Weber barbecue. Pete Lewis and I kept in touch after school, but with time and travel, I lost track of Tom.

A few years ago I visited Pete in Costa Rica, and we were remembering those good times.

"Whatever happened to Tom?" I asked him.

"He moved to Kauai twenty years ago. Raised a great family there."

"I always figured he'd be a great father," I said.

"You know he's Bethany's dad, right?"

"Tom Hamilton is Bethany's dad!? Please give him my regards and aloha!"

When I got back to the Billabong offices a few weeks later, I had a voice message: "Hey, Jim, long time no see. It's Tom. Tom Hamilton. Well...I used to be Tom Hamilton. Now I'm just... *Bethany's dad....*"

Bethany Hamilton's Smoothies

Bethany Hamilton is perhaps mainstream society's best-known female surfer ever, having lost her arm to a shark and gained global fame for her amazing resilience. She's had a Hollywood film (*Soul Surfer*) made about her, been profiled in nearly every major magazine, shares her faith around the world, and wrote a book about diet and fitness. Now she's surfing thirty-foot Jaws, with the grace and dedication that I think comes from her mom and dad.

A Word About Smoothies

A properly made smoothie provides three things any wave lover wants: power, energy, and health. One way to get your veggies is to add them to your smoothie: Throw in spinach, kale, even chopped zucchini or beets. A smoothie made only of orange juice, a few strawberries, and a banana might be tasty, but that's mostly carbohydrates. To make a more complete meal, consider what Laird Hamilton does: add a little protein powder or have a handful of nuts on the side. Also consider including items that are not edible by themselves: turmeric, cinnamon, or a little cocoa powder. Kelly Slater often adds almond milk to the mix. Big-wave legend Ian Walsh adds a superfood botanical supplement. And of course there are countless fruits to consider: watermelon, raspberries, pineapple, mango, tangelos, papaya, pomegranates, grapefruit, apples, cranberries, kiwi, and more.

My favorite smoothie addition is a heaping tablespoon of toasted flax seeds. You can get them at Trader Joe's or almost any health food store. They add a nutty flavor, fiber, and essential nutrients, along with a little crunch and texture.

BETHANY'S PAPAYA NUT SMOOTHIE

Here's one of Bethany's favorite smoothies. She says, "This is not my go-to smoothie but a delicious once-in-a-while treat."

1 fresh papaya

1 frozen banana

1 heaping spoonful peanut butter (or any nut butter)

½ cup canned coconut milk

½ cup almond milk

Ice cubes (optional, if you want it colder)

½ thumb* turmeric root (or ½ teaspoon powder)

½ thumb* ginger root (or ½ teaspoon powder)

* using your own thumb for the measurement

Place all the ingredients in a blender and blend on high speed until smooth.

BETHANY'S AÇAÍ SMOOTHIE

2 packages Sambazon açaí purée

5 ounces Sambazon açaí berry juice

1 small banana

½ cup cut-up fresh pineapple

1 cup organic coconut water, plus more if needed

⅓ cup blueberries

1 tablespoon peanut butter

½ cup coconut flakes (optional)

Place açaí purée, açaí juice, banana, pineapple, coconut water, blueberries, and peanut butter in blender and blend on high speed until smooth. Add more coconut water if necessary, but keep it rather thick. Pour into tall glasses and garnish with coconut flakes if you have some.

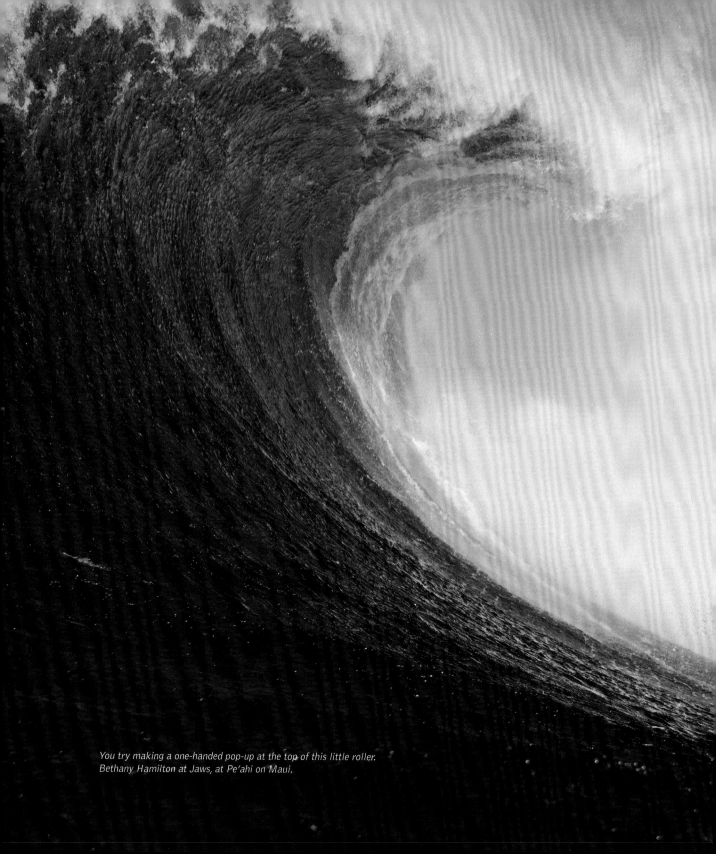

You try making a one-handed pop-up at the top of this little roller.
Bethany Hamilton at Jaws, at Pe'ahi on Maui.

MAKAHA, OAHU
Little Lovely Hula Hands

For years during my tenure as editor at *Surfer,* the North Shore of Oahu was my home for the holidays. Arrival was timed to make Triple Crown impresario Randy Rarick's Halloween party, the social event of the season. I had begun this annual *Surfer* staff sojourn by renting big-wave pioneer and oceanographer Ricky Grigg's log cabin house at … yep, the surf spot called Log Cabins.

My photo editor during most of that era was the illustrious Jeff Divine. Already getting shots in *Surfer* when we were both still at Cal Western University, he was a bona fide surf media veteran at a ripe old twenty-seven. Jeff and Rell Sunn were a couple back then, media darlings in their own right. Rell was the Queen of Makaha, surfing's female global ambassador, the living incarnation of aloha spirit. (Her fabulous daughter Jan Sunn carries on Rell's aloha with her foundation to this day.)

Every Thanksgiving back then, Rell put on a big kalua turkey feast. Beyond being a great dinner party, it was worth attending just to pay respect to the Makaha crew, who stopped in throughout the day to pay homage to the Queen. One year when we arrived, a big Polynesian guy with fingers the size of cigars was sitting in a rocking chair on Rell's front porch, telling stories on the guitar strings. My three-year-old daughter, Kim, with skin the color of pink-white marble and hair like wheat and ripe strawberries, was captivated by his music. In fact, none of us could stop watching; his guitar spoke like magic from a Kahuna.

Mesmerized, I barely noticed that Kim had turned around and run down the steps, out to the lane where the cars were parked. We had recently bought her a little hula outfit, the kind you get in a tourist shop in Waikiki, with a green grass skirt and two coconut shells for a top. It was still in its package in the car. Before we could catch up to her, she'd opened the car door and gotten out her hula costume. I know she'd never seen hula before. But she put her outfit on, walked back up on the porch, stood right in front of him, and started to hula. She obviously wasn't doing a formal hula, but she instinctively put one hand on her hip and moved the other around. Little lovely hula hands.

The big guy just melted. As she moved her hands and feet to the rhythm, he played every hula melody he knew. Some ethereal bond between a royal Hawaiian musician and a three-year-old Celtic princess had formed, and the spell was not to be broken.

Rell came over from where she was manning the barbecue and said, "Jim, Jim, take a picture."

Hula Kim and Henry Kapono

I said, "This is too good, I don't want to spoil it."

She laughed. "That's Henry Kapono. Do you know who he is?"

Did I know who he was? Only the most magical, successful, charismatic Hawaiian musical artist of the era—or maybe ever. Now that I knew that, I was too shy, so Rell snapped the shot. The shaded porch was dark, but the fire from two souls in sync lit the photo: an artist and his muse.

My daughter has a little daughter of her own now, with the same strawberries-and-cream complexion. The image of Kapono and Kim is framed on her wall, signed by him at a show during one of his mainland tours. The hula they shared was one of life's magic moments. As were all of Rell's Thanksgiving dinners.

Rell Sunn's Kalua Turkey

Buffalo Keaulana taught me this mayonnaise trick—it keeps the turkey moist after a long time on the grill. Serve the shredded turkey on a bed of white rice garnished with pineapple spears, and if you're serving it for Thanksgiving, feel free to add all the traditional mainland trimmings.

SERVES 12

¾ cup liquid smoke seasoning, divided

12-pound fresh turkey, insides removed, washed, and patted dry

1 cup coarse Alaea red Hawaiian sea salt

Mayonnaise as needed

1 cup fresh orange juice

Place a generous layer of hardwood charcoal briquettes in a Weber-style grill and light them.

Pour ½ cup liquid smoke seasoning outside and inside turkey, rubbing it into skin to spread it evenly. Rub salt inside cavity and over exterior, including gently under skin. Slather with mayonnaise. Wrap bird snugly in heavy-duty foil.

When coals are hot, move to either side of grill so heat is indirect. Set bird in a disposable aluminum roasting pan. Place on grill, close lid, and roast for 4½ to 5 hours. Every hour or so, add half a dozen briquettes to fire. When done, skin should be slightly crispy and browned, and a thermometer inserted into turkey thigh (not touching bone) should register 170°F. Remove from heat, remove foil, and let turkey rest for about half an hour.

While turkey is resting, strain pan juices into a saucepan. Add remaining ¼ cup liquid smoke and orange juice. Bring to a boil over medium-high heat and cook until it reduces a little but does not thicken, about 10 minutes. Reduce heat to low and keep warm.

Remove skin and bones from turkey. Transfer meat to a large platter.

Shred turkey to consistency of pulled pork. Pour warm pan juices over meat, toss lightly to coat, and serve.

WAIKIKI, HAWAII

Hope & Outriggers

One New Year's Day, three paddlers in a twenty-two-foot Hawaiian outrigger canoe attempted the first assault on giant outside reef waves at a North Shore spot called Avalanche. One of them was Dale Hope. Paddling hard, they dropped into a swell whose slope was nearly twice the length of the canoe. The unsuccessful, nearly disastrous outcome, in which Dale broke his arm, was a feat of bravado still talked about today.

Dale, who wrote the definitive book on the aloha shirt, is a second-generation shirt designer and premier waterman masquerading as a cultural historian. His father was one of the seminal creators of the Hawaiian shirt. A lifelong member of Honolulu's ultra-exclusive Outrigger Canoe Club, Dale hosts me there when I'm in town—usually over an ono poke bowl and a gin gimlet. Although the club was founded in 1908 as a surfing club to provide dressing rooms for men and boys who had no easy access to the good surfing areas of Waikiki, it now champions not only surfing but a dozen other sports. It hosts social activities, has a great bar and food, and provides a view of one of the world's best sunsets.

Dale is the haole version of pure aloha—a man respected in almost all circles of Hawaiian life. He will no doubt be in the history books someday. He's already in mine.

Ono Poke Bowl

Poke (pronounced "poh-kay") is a Hawaiian treat that has become one of the mainland's trendiest items. Its new popularity has imbued Hawaiian chefs (understandably) with a little proprietary jealousy, a sure sign of a long-term food trend. A combo of super-fresh high-grade raw fish, dressing, and spices served in a bowl, it's the perfect starter for a meal or a great high-protein, low-calorie filler. It's fresh, healthy, and fast. Already a staple in California and New York, it's starting to show up on menus around the globe.

SERVES 6

1 pound sashimi-grade tuna, cut into
  jumbo-olive-size cubes
3 tablespoons finely chopped fresh cilantro
2 teaspoons grated fresh ginger
1 small jalapeño, minced (optional)

1 green onion, minced
¼ cup soy sauce
2 tablespoons sesame oil
1 ripe but slightly firm avocado
2 teaspoons sesame seeds or Trader Joe's golden
  roasted flax seeds (my favorite)

Combine tuna, cilantro, ginger, jalapeño (if using), green onion, soy sauce and sesame oil in a bowl; toss gently. Cover and refrigerate for at least 1 hour or up to 3 hours.

Just before serving, peel and pit avocado and cut into small cubes. Combine with tuna mixture, making sure avocado is well integrated with tuna. Scoop poke into 6 bowls, sprinkle with sesame or flax seeds, and serve.

HONOLULU, OAHU

Chart House: A Legendary Original

In 1961, Hawaiian surfing star Joey Cabell founded the Chart House with big-wave legend Buzzy Bent. A member of Duke Kahanamoku's personal surf team and perhaps the greatest speed stylist of his generation, Cabell turned the Chart House into a phenomenon. The idea was to serve fresh fish, teriyaki-marinated steaks, and the most bountiful salad bar the world had ever seen. The Chart House was an immediate success, spawning a host of imitators. Great views of a waterfront combined with baseball-cut sirloin steaks, bottomless salad bars, and tropical cocktails might seem obvious today, but it was revolutionary then.

This model of casual yet elegant dining became the new standard for waterfront destinations. Waiters surfed all day, and then donned their reverse-print Reyn Spooner shirts to sit at your table and chat about the waves and weather as they took your order. And the bartenders at the Chart House held serious status in the surf culture. It quickly grew into a small chain, eventually becoming one of the most successful upscale ocean-themed restaurant chains in the world. Although Cabell's Waikiki location no longer has a salad bar, it does have a number of fabulous signature salads. He basically invented the modern salad bar, which is now ubiquitous.

Cabell still oversees his Waikiki Chart House. You can find him at dawn at the harbor picking out the best seafood for the evening's menu. His amazing wife, Yana, gives the restaurant a warmth that the loyal regulars cherish. It is old Hawaii—with just the right touch of new—at its finest.

Sunset dreams at the Waikiki Chart House

Salad Bar

The Chart House may not have invented the salad bar, but it reinvented it as a more elaborate cornucopia of fresh ingredients. Creating your own elaborate salad bar for a party is actually pretty simple, and it's a sure crowd-pleaser, especially with a health-conscious guest list.

In large separate bowls, place as many of the following as you can get: spinach, green leaf lettuce, chopped romaine, shredded cabbage, and butter lettuce.

Fill medium-size bowls with such things as sliced mushrooms, shredded carrots, kale, chopped red bell peppers, garbanzo beans, sliced celery, slivered onions, bean sprouts, artichoke hearts, and sliced yellow squash.

Next, fill small bowls with as many of these as you like: olives, chopped tomatoes, chopped green onions, parmesan, feta and blue cheeses, croutons, and walnuts.

Ladle blue cheese and ranch dressings into bowls, and put out a bottle of herb vinaigrette. If you like, add a plate of grilled chicken, crumbled bacon bits, and/or grilled shrimp for the carnivores. Then invite your guests to concoct the salad of their dreams.

MAKAWAO, MAUI

Surfing Cowboy Volleyball

I learned about the world's best steak from Maui firefighters and cowboys when I attended Mauna'olu College. If you wanted beef, there was only one place to go on that side of the island: Makawao. A few miles up the road past the former Mauna'olu campus, it's still an old upcountry paniolo (cowboy) town, but now rental cars tie up to the hitching posts instead of horses. I got to know some of the good folks in Makawao because I played on the college volleyball team. There were no other schools nearby, so we competed against the fire department and cowboy teams. After games, we'd all go to the Makawao Steak House and drink beer, listen to Hawaiian slide guitar, eat slabs of ribeye, and laugh like hyenas. Substitute a drawl for the pidgin English, and you could just as well be in Fort Worth.

Porterhouse Steak with Herbed Butter & Portuguese Chimichurri

My friend Rodney "Handsome Bugga" Kilborn is a retired fireman who lives in Kula, Maui, runs most of the island's surf contests, and has a mean way with a grill. I suspect firefighters understand hot coals the way cowboys understand beef. He told me once the only problem with this dish is that five or six days later you'll be hungry again.

One thing the local cowboys confirmed was my dad's sage opinion of beef cuts: filet mignon (or tenderloin) is the most tender; ribeye (or spencer) is the most flavorful; and strip steak (or New York) is right in between. The cowboys introduced me to the porterhouse—a tenderloin and a piece of strip steak separated by a T-shaped bone—and it was a beefeater's revelation. Hawaiians like to eat, cowboys know their cuts—and porterhouse is a serious hunk of meat.

Okay, this isn't low calorie. But as Julia Child once said, "The only time to eat diet food is while you're waiting for the steak to cook."

SERVES 6

2 tablespoons finely ground coriander
2 tablespoons roasted, mashed fresh garlic
2 tablespoons sweet red paprika
1 tablespoon Alaea red Hawaiian sea salt
1 tablespoon freshly ground black pepper
1 teaspoon onion powder

1 teaspoon garlic powder
1 teaspoon dried oregano, crumbled
6 porterhouse steaks (about 1¾ pounds each)
Portuguese Chimichurri (*recipe follows*)
Herb Butter (*recipe follows*)

Combine coriander, garlic, paprika, salt, pepper, onion powder, garlic powder, and oregano in a small bowl and mix well. Rub on both sides of steaks. Set aside until meat comes to room temperature, about 30 minutes.

Light a charcoal grill and bring to medium heat or preheat a gas grill to 350°F. When grill is hot, place steaks on grill, making sure tenderloin sides are farthest from direct heat. Cook for 5 to 6 minutes per side for rare, or until done to taste.

Transfer to a platter or individual plates. Drizzle a little Portuguese Chimichurri sauce on fillets and spread a little Herb Butter on strip steaks. Serve extra sauce in bowls for guests to add as they want.

PORTUGUESE CHIMICHURRI

½ small onion, minced
3 cloves garlic, minced
1 teaspoon lemon juice
½ teaspoon paprika
½ cup minced fresh basil,
   preferably opal variety

½ cup minced fresh cilantro
2 tablespoons minced fresh oregano
⅓ cup Spanish extra-virgin olive oil
2 tablespoons red wine vinegar

In a medium bowl, stir together onion, garlic, lemon juice, paprika, basil, cilantro, and oregano. Whisk in oil and vinegar until mixture has a thick, sauce-like texture.

HERB BUTTER

This is a kitchen staple that's also great with chicken, seafood, and vegetables.

¾ cup (1½ sticks) unsalted butter,
   softened until very soft
¼ cup snipped fresh chives (¼ inch long)
½ cup minced fresh parsley
1 tablespoon Worcestershire sauce
Sea salt and freshly ground pepper, to taste

In a small bowl with a lid, stir together all ingredients until well combined. Cover and keep refrigerated until needed.

TURTLE BAY, NORTH SHORE, OAHU
Lei Lei's Yea Yea's

Despite efforts by numerous drinking establishments on Oahu's North Shore, Lei Lei's at the Turtle Bay Resort has remained the favorite of locals and surfers alike for more than a decade. At the risk of ruining a good thing, I give it a gold star for the best service and most humble, genuine vibe of any surfer bar in the world. On any off-contest night during the Triple Crown of Surfing, half the world-tour pros will be in the bar. The other half are usually on their way to or from.

I'm not saying it's the best watering hole ever, but I once commandeered a golf cart on the way out of Lei Lei's, overfilled it with passengers, drove it 200 yards to the Turtle Bay parking lot, artfully evaded hotel security, parked it in the space my own car had been in, drove a friend to Pupukea, returned home... and didn't remember any of it. Although some friends apparently do.

The lush life on Oahu's North Shore, near Waimea Bay

The "Maitai" Mai Tai

Although the mai tai didn't originate in Hawaii, it was invented by aficionados of all things South Pacific in California tiki bars in honor of the Islands. Legend has it that when Trader Vic made the drink for a guest from Tahiti, she took one sip and yelled, "Maitai roa ae!"—meaning—"Out of this world—the best!"

This recipe is the real deal. Its roots trace to both Don the Beachcomber in the 1930s and Victor "Trader Vic" Bergeron Jr.'s 1944 recipe, and it also pays homage to the Royal Hawaiian and Moana Hotel versions from 1953. And, of course, Lei Lei's serves a mean rendition.

Note: Orgeat is a syrup made from whole blanched almonds. The almond oil gives it a richness that you can't get from syrup made with almond flavoring.

MAKES 1 COCKTAIL

1 cup crushed ice
1 jigger (1½ ounces) spiced rum
1 jigger (1½ ounces) coconut-flavored rum
2 ounces pineapple juice

2 ounces orange juice
1½ teaspoons orgeat
1 tablespoon dark rum
 float

In a cocktail mixer full of ice, combine the spiced rum, coconut-flavored rum, pineapple juice, orange juice, and orgeat. Shake well, strain into a bucket glass, and float the dark rum on top. Garnish with a mint sprig. Or cherry. Or pineapple wedge. Or lime slice. Or whatever. You can't go wrong. The Royal Hawaiian has seven versions. Whatever you choose, skip the freaking parasol—otherwise you'll miss the green flash at sunset.

HONOLUA BAY, MAUI
Nightmare in Red

For many years, the crumpled carcass of a wrecked automobile lay at the foot of the cliff at Honolua Bay. It was a sober reminder not to park too close to the edge.

One night photographer Eric Aeder and friends camped on the cliff in the pineapple field. The plan was to join us for an early-morning surf. Around midnight a rainstorm came up, plowing the fine red dirt into slippery sludge. In the middle of the downpour, the other campers woke to Eric's panicked screams: "Get out, get out now! The car is sliding off the cliff!"

There was no time to think. Ken McKnight (nicknamed "animal man" for his surf intensity) slung open the back door and dove headfirst into the thick crimson mire. The others followed. Drenched, caked with mud, spitting red granules from his mouth, Ken rose to his feet to inspect the carnage. But the car hadn't moved. They were all safe. It seemed impossible. Rounding the front of the car, they looked inside. Sprawled on the front seat was Eric, arms waving, still screaming "Get out!" in a dead sleep.

Korean Short Ribs

This is an updated version of the meat that would have been part of the plate lunch Buzzy enjoyed. Eating it on an open beam eight stories up is not recommended.

SERVES 6

3 pounds short ribs, cut in ½-inch slices across the bones (flanken-style)

⅓ cup soy sauce

⅓ cup brown sugar

⅓ cup rice wine

1 tablespoon sesame oil

2 teaspoons freshly ground black pepper

¼ teaspoon cayenne

1 medium onion, peeled and quartered

8 cloves garlic, peeled

1 small Asian pear, peeled, cored, and quartered (or other pear or tart apple)

½ teaspoon minced fresh ginger

2 teaspoons sesame seeds

Rinse short ribs in cold water, pat dry, and place in a wide, shallow bowl. In another bowl, mix together soy sauce, brown sugar, rice wine, sesame oil, black pepper, and cayenne.

Put onion, garlic, pear, and ginger in the work bowl of a food processor. Grind ingredients to a smooth purée, then add to soy sauce mixture. Add sesame seeds. Thin with ¼ cup water.

Pour marinade over short ribs and mix well. Cover and refrigerate for at least 2 hours, or overnight.

Bring short ribs to room temperature, drain, and discard marinade. Cook short ribs on a hot grill or under the broiler for 2 to 3 minutes per side, until nicely browned but juicy. Pile grilled meat on a plate and add traditional plate lunch items (see below).

Plate Lunch

If you've been to Hawaii even once, you know the plate lunch. If not, it's a hearty combo-plate lunch that usually involves two big scoops (rice and macaroni "salad"), a little green salad, and hearty helpings of meat or poultry. Here's what to assemble for your own good plate lunch.

Korean Short Ribs (see recipe above)

½ cup Kalua Pork (see recipe page 21)

1 scoop cooked and cooled brown rice

1 scoop cooked and cooled macaroni with lowfat mayonnaise

Small green salad

1 small sliced chile (any kind)

Ssamjang (spicy Korean soybean paste), for dipping (optional)

2 teaspoons (2 packets) soy sauce

Taking the Drop

Buzzy Trent is credited for the memorable quote, "Big waves are not measured in size, they are measured in increments of fear." When he was not setting early benchmarks for courage and daring in the previously unridden waves at Makaha and Sunset Beach, the legendary big-wave rider worked construction on the high-rise hotels that now line Waikiki like a forest of cement koa. Miki Dora once told me this story, and Paul Strauch (another legendary surfer from the early '60s) confirmed it.

Buzzy was up on the twelfth floor of a construction site putting the skeleton of steel girders into place. A coworker accidentally swung a beam and hit him in the back, knocking him off the ledge. On the free fall, Buzzy somehow managed to grab onto a horizontal crossbeam a couple of stories down—breaking his fall—and then grabbed the next beam down and held on. Still eight stories up and on an exposed eight-inch crossbeam, he walked across it into the construction elevator, went down, and got his lunch. He rode back up, gave the coworker a good crack on the head, and then sat down calmly to eat his plate lunch.

MEXICO
A Coastline of Waves, Wanderers & Eating Traditions

Mexico was once to Californian beach lovers what Indonesia was to Australians: a big, wide-open frontier, with uncrowded surf, beautiful coastlines, and cheap, delicious food. During my college years and early surf sojourns, I combed the coasts of both Baja's gnarled finger and the mainland's plusher tropics, relishing the food as much as the waves.

Norteamericanos often forget how varied Mexican cooking is. It goes far beyond tacos to span an amazing array of dishes that unite to form one of the world's great cuisines. In the coastal towns, chefs married indigenous staples with Emperor Maximilian's French sauces; elsewhere, they mixed Spanish traditions with Mayan methodology. *Pescado veracruzana* and *chiles en nogada*, for example, are not the fare gringos are accustomed to, and they are a delightful surprise to those who haven't explored beyond the Sonoran bean burrito. From the fish tacos invented in Ensenada's harbor, to the ancient moles and pipianes of Oaxaca and Michoacán, from the tubes of Puerto Escondido to the long Baja points at Abreojos and Pequeña, Mexico's recipes and waves still offer up discoveries and delights.

California's big-wave riders cut their teeth here on Isla Todos Santos, Baja California.

Classic Caesar Salad 157

Chiles en Nogada 158
Beef-and-Fruit-Stuffed Poblanos with Walnut Sauce

Enchiladas Puerto Escondido 161

Pozole 162

Pescado Veracruzana 165

Machaca & Eggs 167

Avocados Stuffed with Jumbo Shrimp 173

Doña Victoria's Kahlúa Coconut Flan 174

Baja bound: Curious Gabe and his VW camper

TIJUANA, BAJA CALIFORNIA
Hail Caesar!

One of the most popular first courses on American menus, the Caesar salad, was invented in Mexico, although not by a Mexican. The man credited with its creation—Caesar Cardini—was an Italian immigrant who moved his restaurant from California to Tijuana in 1924, during Prohibition, so he could sell alcohol. His place was a hit from the beginning, and once Caesar became known for his salad and the tableside tossing technique he devised, it took off like margaritas, fish tacos, and Corona beer would do in the decades to come.

Caesar's Restaurante has since had different owners, but it's still there today, in the original building. And despite what you hear about violence from drug gangs, Tijuana is still as safe for visitors as any big city in the US. It's worth a stop on your next trip to Baja to sample a little culinary history.

Classic Caesar Salad

The egg yolks are what give richness to the emulsion, and the anchovies provide a briny flavor that's hard to substitute.

SERVES 6

2 anchovy fillets packed in oil, drained and minced

1 small clove garlic, minced

2 large egg yolks

2 tablespoons fresh lemon juice, plus more for seasoning

¾ teaspoon Dijon mustard

2 tablespoons extra-virgin olive oil

½ cup vegetable oil

¼ cup finely grated parmesan, plus freshly shaved parmesan for serving

Sea salt and freshly ground black pepper, to taste

3 romaine hearts, washed, dried, and leaves separated

Homemade Croutons (*recipe follows*)

Combine minced anchovies and garlic on a cutting board, using the side of a knife blade to mash them into a paste. Scrape mixture into a medium bowl and whisk in egg yolks, lemon juice, and mustard until fully combined. Gradually whisk in olive oil, then vegetable oil; keep whisking until dressing is thick and glossy. Sprinkle in ¼ cup parmesan, and season to taste with salt, pepper, and more lemon juice to taste.

Cut lettuce leaves cut in half and place in serving bowl. Gently toss lettuce, croutons, and dressing, then top with parmesan shavings.

HOMEMADE CROUTONS

Make your own! Tearing, not cutting, the bread results in nooks and crannies that better catch the dressing and add texture.

3 cups torn 1-inch pieces country bread, with crusts

3 tablespoons extra-virgin olive oil

Sea salt and freshly ground pepper, to taste

Preheat oven to 375°F. Arrange torn bread on a baking sheet and drizzle with olive oil. Season to taste with salt and pepper. Bake, tossing occasionally, until golden, 10 to 15 minutes.

Chiles en Nogada
Beef-and-Fruit-Stuffed Poblanos with Walnut Sauce

When Margarita's Village opened, we hired some family members from Olamendi's, one of the finest restaurants—and families—in Orange County. They cooked the food we'd tasted on surf trips to different regions of Mexico.

Much of the Mexican food we eat in the US comes from only half a dozen of the thirty-one states in Mexico. Culinarily, Mexico resembles the European Union, where each state has its own dishes. These *chiles en nogada* are commonly found in Oaxaca and Guerrero. Originally made to celebrate Mexican Independence Day on September 16, this stuffed chile has always been a favorite of mine. In Mexico they use pork, but my friends at Olamendi's use ground beef, and I like the result better.

SERVES 12

2 tablespoons canola oil
½ onion, finely chopped
½ pound lean ground beef
2 cloves garlic, minced
2 plum tomatoes, cored, peeled, and
   finely chopped

2 tablespoons finely chopped parsley
½ cup beef broth
6 tablespoons raisins
2 tablespoons finely chopped blanched almonds
1 small ripe plantain or banana, peeled
   and finely chopped

WALNUT SAUCE

6 ounces walnut pieces
¾ cup milk
6 ounces queso fresco

1 cup sour cream
3 tablespoons sugar
2 tablespoons sherry

CHILES

12 poblano chiles
1 cup all-purpose flour
5 large eggs, separated
2 tablespoons kosher salt

1 tablespoon distilled white vinegar
2 cups canola oil, for frying
1 tablespoon pomegranate seeds

Heat oil in a large skillet over medium heat. Sauté onion until soft, about 8 minutes. Add ground beef and sauté, stirring occasionally, until cooked through. Add garlic and cook for 1 minute more. Add tomatoes and parsley and cook about 5 minutes.

Pour beef broth into pan and spoon in raisins, almonds, and plantain. Cook, stirring, until mixture is thick, about 10 minutes. Transfer to a bowl, season to taste, and set aside.

To make the walnut sauce, place walnuts in a 2-quart saucepan. Add milk and bring to a simmer. Let sit, covered, for about 30 minutes while nuts soften. When soft, transfer walnuts to a blender and add milk, queso fresco, sour cream, sugar, and sherry. Purée until very smooth and thick, at least 2 minutes. Transfer to a nonreactive bowl, cover, and refrigerate for 15 to 30 minutes to cool it down.

When you're ready to prepare the final dish, heat a charcoal or gas grill to high heat/425°F. Place poblanos on a heavy-duty aluminum foil sheet on grill and char, carefully turning with tongs, until blackened all over, about 20 minutes. Transfer to a baking sheet and let cool. Peel and discard skins, stems, and seeds, and cut a slit down the length of each chile. Remove seeds and ribs, taking care to keep chiles intact. Spoon 2 to 3 tablespoons of beef filling into each chile. Carefully close chile around filling.

Spread flour on another baking sheet covered with foil. In a large bowl, beat egg whites until soft peaks form; whisk in egg yolks, salt, and vinegar. Carefully dredge each chile in flour, shaking off excess, and then coat in egg batter.

Heat oil in a 12-inch skillet over medium-high heat. Place a few chiles in oil, being careful not to crowd skillet, and fry, flipping once, until golden brown and filling is heated through, about 5 minutes. Using a slotted spoon, transfer to paper towels to drain. Repeat until all chiles are fried.

While still hot, place on serving plates and spoon walnut sauce over poblanos, coating completely. Sprinkle with pomegranate seeds and serve.

PUERTO ESCONDIDO, OAXACA
The Once-Hidden Big-Wave Port of Call

Puerto Escondido remained a quiet fishing village long after being first visited by surfers as early as 1959. Photos of giant hollow tubes began circulating among the core wave seekers in the early '70s. Christened the "Mexican Pipeline" for its size, hollowness, and power, it became a new gauntlet thrown down to big-wave aficionados. Universally accepted as the world's most challenging sand-bottom break, it has become a proving ground for spectacular tube riding in massive barrels. The village of "Puerto" has grown over the years, with one of the few improvements being the proliferation of excellent restaurants.

Greg Long is a frequent visitor here—he has won more than one XXL Big Wave Award for slaying these monsters. Besides being considered one of (if not *the*) most accomplished big-wave riders of his generation, Greg has become surfing's premier ambassador to the world at large. Handsome, articulate, humble, and thoughtful, he has assumed the mantle from Shaun Tomson—and he wears it well. The recipe here is one of Greg's favorites.

Enchiladas Puerto Escondido

On an early trip to Puerto Escondido, our surf crew ordered enchiladas. We were awed by the appearance of a huge clay-oven dish holding more than thirty rolled tortillas. That didn't stop the five of us from demolishing the platter in less time than it takes to paddle through a monster set at the local beach break.

SERVES 6

4 (14.5-ounce) cans fire-roasted tomatoes

4 large boneless, skinless chicken breasts

1 (4-ounce) can green chiles, drained and diced

½ medium onion, diced

4 cups prepared enchilada sauce

12 (10-inch) corn tortillas

4 cups grated Mexican cheese (Asadero, Oaxaca, and/or substitute Monterey Jack)

1 cup light sour cream

½ cup crumbled queso fresco

1 large avocado, peeled, pitted, and sliced into 12 pieces

12 pitted black olives

2 green onions, diced

Coarsely chopped fresh cilantro, for garnish

Preheat oven to 350°F.

Place roasted tomatoes in a large pot over medium-high heat. Add chicken breasts. Bring to a boil, then reduce heat to medium-low and simmer gently for 30 minutes. Remove chicken with slotted spoon to a work bowl. Shred with a fork or by hand into 1-inch strips. Add green chiles and onion to shredded chicken and toss until well combined.

Coat a large baking dish with oil or cooking spray. Put 2 cups enchilada sauce in a shallow bowl. Dip 1 tortilla in sauce, shake off excess, and lay out tortilla on a cutting board or plate. Spoon $1/12$th of chicken mixture onto it. Top with about ¼ cup grated cheese. Fold ends of tortilla over filled center. Place tortilla seam side down into oiled baking dish. Repeat until all tortillas have been filled. Pour remaining enchilada sauce over assembled enchiladas and top with remaining grated cheese.

Bake until cheese has melted thoroughly, about 20 minutes. Remove from oven and spoon a dollop of sour cream and crumbled queso fresco on each enchilada. Top each with a slice of avocado and an olive. Garnish with green onions and cilantro.

Pozole

Pozole is traditionally a Sunday soup, a solid, simple broth with nutritious ingredients and a plateful of herbs and spices to customize it to your liking. As an added bonus, it has a reputation as a cure for a hard night.

SERVES 6

1 pound boneless, skinless chicken breasts
2 pounds fresh pork belly, cut in 2-inch chunks
2 pounds pork shoulder, cut in 2-inch chunks
Sea salt and freshly ground pepper, to taste
1 large yellow onion, peeled, halved, and stuck
   with 2 cloves
1 bay leaf
1 tablespoon chopped fresh garlic
2 teaspoons toasted cumin seeds

3 ounces dried red New Mexico chiles
   (about 10 large chiles)
1½ pounds dried hominy, soaked overnight
   in water and drained
1 cup shredded cabbage
½ cup thinly sliced radishes
2 cups finely diced white onion
Lime wedges
Roughly chopped fresh cilantro, to taste
Toasted Mexican oregano, to taste

Place chicken breast in large soup pot, cover with 10 cups water, and bring to boil over high heat. Reduce heat to low and simmer for 20 minutes.

Remove chicken from broth with a slotted spoon. Let it cool slightly, shred it, and set it aside. Add pork belly, pork shoulder, onion with cloves, bay leaf, garlic, and cumin to broth. Simmer for 1 hour.

While soup is simmering, toast dried chiles lightly in cast-iron skillet or stovetop griddle until just fragrant. Remove and discard stems and seeds. Put chiles in saucepan over low heat and cover with 4 cups water. Simmer 30 minutes and let cool. In blender, purée chiles and their liquid to a smooth paste with roughly the consistency of yogurt. Pour purée through a strainer and set aside.

When pork has cooked in the broth for an hour, add drained hominy to stockpot. Simmer for 30 minutes more, until meat is tender and hominy has softened. Skim and discard fat from surface of broth. Stir in reserved shredded chicken and 1 cup chile purée and simmer for 10 more minutes to heat through. Taste and add salt and pepper if needed.

To serve, place some cabbage and radish slices into 6 wide soup bowls. Ladle in pozole. Set out additional cabbage and radishes, diced onion, lime wedges, cilantro, and oregano in small dishes, and let guests garnish their pozole as they like.

SHIPWRECKS, SAN JOSÉ DEL CABO
Keep Your Motor Running

My friend and colleague Tom Servais is a legendary sportsman. He can surf Tavarua, mountain bike down Top of the World, stand-up paddle in Indonesia, snowboard off-piste in Whistler, and drive all night to windsurf Jalama. He plays a mean game of tennis and an even meaner game of backgammon. He's also one of the best lensmen in the surf industry.

One day some years back, we were racing to the Tijuana airport on our way to a week near Shipwrecks outside Cabo San Lucas. We were late, and the snarling traffic in Tijuana only made the situation more dire. "I don't think we're going to make it," Tom said, looking at his watch.

Blasting up to the front of the terminal, we leaped out of the car. The flight was due to leave in less than ten minutes. We were in a no-parking zone with no boarding passes—an absolute missed-flight situation in any California airport, even back before 9/11 and TSA tightening. At the time, Mexicans had a different mind-set. As I shoved a wad of pesos at them, porters grabbed our boards, bags, and Tom's windsurfing gear and took off running, clearing the aisles for us as we sprinted for the gate. They split off at one point to rush our gear out to the underbelly of the plane. Now it was only a matter of seconds.

"They're holding the plane for us!" Tom was almost laughing as we rushed the gate, handed off our tickets, bounded through the airplane's doors, and careened into two empty seats, drenched in sweat but relieved.

In less than a minute the plane lifted off, and we watched the broad ramble of the border city recede into miniature as we caught our breath. A moment later, Tom got this funny look on his face. He looked over at me and asked, very slowly, "Hey...what did you do with the car?"

Pescado Veracruzana

SERVES 6

½ cup lemon juice (preferably fresh)

3 tablespoons extra-virgin olive oil

6 red snapper fillets, 6 ounces each

2 large white onions, sliced into ¼-inch strips

2 medium green bell peppers, sliced into ¼-inch strips

1 medium yellow bell pepper, sliced into ¼-inch strips

6 fire-roasted tomatoes, quartered

1 small roasted chile pepper, minced

½ cup sweet white wine

½ cup nonpareil capers, drained

3 tablespoons tomato paste

3 cloves garlic, slivered (about ¼ cup)

½ teaspoon ground cumin

½ teaspoon dried oregano

Sea salt and freshly ground pepper, to taste

2 to 3 dried bay leaves

3 to 4 sprigs fresh thyme

6 tablespoons chopped fresh cilantro

Whisk together lemon juice and olive oil in a large bowl and add fish. Cover and marinate in the refrigerator for at least 30 minutes.

Preheat oven to 375°F. Lightly oil a 12-inch skillet and sauté onions and bell peppers over high heat for 3 minutes. Add tomatoes and chile pepper, cooking for another 2 to 3 minutes. Mix in white wine, capers, tomato paste, garlic, cumin, oregano, salt, and pepper, and continue to cook over low heat until sauce begins to form, about 3 minutes.

Lightly oil bottom of a large roasting pan. Cover bottom of pan with half of sauce. Remove fish from marinade, and arrange fillets over sauce. Scatter bay leaves and thyme over fish, then pour remaining sauce over fish.

Bake just until flesh flakes when tested with the tip of a knife, 15 to 20 minutes. Use a spatula to transfer fish to a platter or individual plates, and ladle sauce and cooking juices over fillets. Scatter cilantro over top. Serve with white rice and a side of sautéed Mexican crookneck squash.

PUNTA PERFECTA, CABO SAN LUCAS
Priorities in Place

One year at the annual Surf Industry Manufacturers Association conference in Cabo San Lucas, Quiksilver's CEO, Bob McKnight, gave the opening remarks. It was a well-attended kick-off dinner—Bob was the surf industry's most important and respected executive, and Quiksilver was at the zenith of its reign as the top brand in surfing.

Bob's speech was notable to me less for what he said and more for what he did right after his talk. Before the clapping had finished, he slid over to my table and asked, "Is there any way I can get a ride with you out to surf Punta Perfecta tomorrow?"

No question could have better cemented the authenticity of the surf world's most successful mogul—the priority is to surf the best wave we can find. Like many other surf-brand executives, Bob is a solid, passionate wave rider. The next day, he distinguished himself at a cliff-sheltered lineup that was worth the two-hour daybreak drive over rutted dirt roads to an isolated spot with head-high waves.

One of Bob's other most admirable traits is that he can hold his own. Whether he's at a black-tie dinner or a campfire in Bali, he loves the food and drink—but never overdoes it. The same goes for his surfing. From a small, sloppy beach break to big point surf, he gets there early and gets his share—but never more. Bob built a billion-dollar empire on the credo he exhibited that night in Cabo: Surfing is a way of life, and people will buy it if you live it. To do that successfully, you don't just have salt water in your heart—you have it in your veins.

Machaca & Eggs

Nothing is quite as satisfying on a scorching drive back from a good Baja surf session as pulling over at some little shack along the highway and getting a plate of good food and a cold beer. I've had many memorable meals with Bob McKnight, but this machaca stands out because it was a true getaway—we lost all phone connection and found great waves.

Machaca is a hearty, homey shredded-beef concoction commonly served with eggs for breakfast. But it works at any time of the day—or night.

SERVES 6

3 cups diced white onion
1 green bell pepper, diced
¾ cup vegetable oil, divided
1½ pounds beef or skirt steak, roasted and shredded
¼ cup beef broth
½ teaspoon paprika
½ teaspoon ground cumin
¼ teaspoon garlic powder

¼ teaspoon dried oregano
3 large ripe tomatoes, roughly chopped
6 fresh serrano chiles, finely chopped
9 large eggs, lightly beaten
12 sprigs fresh cilantro
1 large avocado, peeled, pitted, and cut into 12 thin slices
6 tablespoons sour cream

In a large skillet over medium-high heat, sauté onion and bell pepper in 3 tablespoons oil until softened, then add beef and brown it, stirring, over high heat.

Put broth in a small bowl and stir in paprika, cumin, garlic powder, and oregano. Pour seasoned broth into skillet, reducing heat to low. Add tomatoes and chiles, and sauté until mixture absorbs most of the moisture, about 15 minutes.

Whisk in eggs and cook briefly, just until the eggs set, then transfer to a platter or serve from individual plates. Garnish with sprigs of fresh cilantro, avocado slices, and a dollop of sour cream, and serve with wheat tortillas and refried beans.

BAJA NORTE
Seven Sisters

The famous Seven Sisters is a string of right-hand point breaks stretching from Punta Cono south to Punta Rosarito. In the shallow tide pools and cobbled ledges there are shellfish, and on the bare bluffs there's room to pitch camp with a view and a fire. Along the dozens of miles of crescent bays, strong south winds create an icy upwelling that turns the water cold and turquoise near the shore and shiny lapis on the horizon. In late winter, the ocean temperature is sometimes ten degrees colder than in San Diego.

Scorpion Bay

Automobiles grind on unpaved roads past rocky headlands, and afterward the cactus trees wear a thin layer of dust. The surfers clustered in the lineups often wear an extra layer of neoprene; when the sky is gray, they add hoods and booties.

Just as sisters share similar characteristics, these points mirror the recurring shape of rocky outcroppings covered by different depths of sand. The cursive shoreline invites repetitive refraction, waves that bend around and down the points. In the same way, Mexico's northern desert dishes are related by the common kinship of carnitas (twice-cooked pork), which is cradled by various enclosures. While each wave and food item carries similarities, each also has a distinct set of traits.

Here are seven exceptional surf points and seven hand-held dishes, each of which uses carnitas as its base.

Punta Cono

A right point that breaks best on winter west swells. Shaped like a fishhook, the swell lines bend 180 degrees, fanning out into long walls across a sheltered bay.

Torta: This is the Mexican version of a Cuban sandwich. Toast a baguette or crusty bread and add carnitas, black beans, avocado, sliced tomato, and cotija cheese. Put on a hot griddle or skillet,

and press with a hot skillet or heavy-duty lid to grill it on both sides.

Punta Maria

An outstanding right point reef break. It needs a west or northwest swell.

Flautas: Load pork and queso Chihuahua (or cheddar) into a flour tortilla, roll it up, and fry in oil. Top with salsa verde. If you campfire cook, try frying the flautas in breakfast bacon drippings. Not the healthiest, but you can't beat the flavor. A Corona longneck is mandatory for accompanying this item.

Punta Negra

A right point reef break with terraced rip-rap behind the swath of sand. It takes a west or northwest swell. The little town looks like a set from a Western movie, and the yellow taqueria on the corner makes a great enchilada.

Enchilada: Fill tortillas with carnitas, red sauce, and Oaxacan (or Monterey Jack) cheese; fold up and bake in oven or cast-iron skillet with lid; top with green onions and sour cream.

Punta Rocosa

A right rock reef point that needs a strong west or northwest swell, but it goes left as well as right and works with a short board or long. There's a perfect camp spot on the south side of the cliffs.

Burrito: Load a large tortilla with carnitas, pinto beans, cotija cheese, adobo sauce, fresh crema, and pico de gallo. Fold up on both ends and roll into a burrito. Wrap wax paper or a napkin around the bottom to protect from leaks.

Punta Santa Rosalillita

A little fishing village with a perfect right point break that works best on a big west swell. To get completely away from the crowds, head to Bahia Santa Rosalillita down the shore, where empty reefs abound. Hurry, though; construction on a marina has already begun.

Tacos al pastor: Load up some carnitas, chopped chile in adobo, diced fresh tomatoes, and pineapple salsa into corn tortillas.

Punta Rosarito

Eighteen miles south of Rosalillita, the point also known as "the Wall" is a consistent right that breaks best on west and northwest swells. It's known for size and power. Keep an eye on the wind, though.

Tostada: Fry a tortilla flat in a pan until crispy, and pile on carnitas, refried beans, shredded lettuce, queso fresco, and guacamole salsa. Try not to woof it in one bite.

ENSENADA

Toasting with Hot Peppers, Cuervo & Hussong's

Odes to Forgotten Scenes South of the Border Down Mexico Way

There are two undeniable, irreplaceable northern Baja contributions to surf cuisine: fish tacos and Corona beer. Nobody anywhere ever produced a tastier taco than the deep-fried fish fillets wrapped in a fresh corn tortilla and topped with cabbage, onions, a dash of hot sauce, and a thin, creamy mayonnaise that makes this concoction irresistible. After a day out at Todos Santos Island when it's big, standing on the Ensenada pier with a hot, crunchy fish taco and a cold Corona—a lime stuck in the longneck—is as good as it gets. Unless you count going to Hussong's.

Hussong's Cantina in Ensenada has always been a mandatory stop for any surfer worth his salt on the rim of a tequila glass. Allegedly inventing the margarita in 1941, this green-and-white clapboard watering hole can at least claim to have served more of them than anyone else. On long

road trips down to Baja's point surf, it's long been obligatory to swig at least a couple of cocktails at the most famous drinking establishment on the upper peninsula. Although each year it becomes a little more commercial, on any weekend this veritable tequila dive has more stories than a New York skyscraper.

The Newport to Ensenada International Yacht Race—California's longest-running and largest sailing event—has been an excuse for one of the town's biggest yearly fiestas, when 270 boats pile into the Ensenada harbor. Hobie Alter's older son, Jeff, once captained his sailboat to a first-place trophy in the last mile through dead-wind maneuvering. Only a true and gracious sailor can downplay winning a race like that. There were a few Cuervo shots that night.

One crew you don't want to get into a drinking match with was my Mexican partners at our Margarita's Village restaurant. At a wedding rehearsal dinner at the Bahia Hotel in Ensenada one night, these Latin locos challenged some of us to a macho duel: giving "hot pepper toasts"—eating jalapeños whole and chasing them with a tequila shot. After six toasts, all of us were sweating profusely, hiccuping uncontrollably, and spinning like swivel sails. By dessert time, we'd moved from giving toasts to being toast.

Not recommended. Even when attending weddings. *Especially* when attending weddings.

The fast right-hander at Salsipuedes, near Ensenada

ZIHUATANEJO, GUERRERO

Gringo Gordo: Surfers' Home Away from Home

Dennis Doyle was a three-time East Coast champ back in the day. We became great friends during our college years, and he became a fixture at San Diego's Sunset Cliffs. He shaped boards, did some funny business, paid his dues, and became an amazing chef. Denny catered my wedding anniversary and got fifteen additional jobs from attendees. For years he owned a little place called El Gringo Gordo in Zihuatanejo, a coastal zone with some of the best surf in mainland Mexico. Every gringo within fifty miles ate at El Gringo Gordo at least twice a week.

All over the world—wherever the waves are good and surfers convene—you'll find little spots like that, where a local or an expat opens a place that caters to traveling surfers: Caliche's Wishbone in Jaco, Costa Rica; Rock Food in Hossegor, France; the Balcony or Old Man's in Bali; Rotherham's Punta Roca in El Salvador; and Kitchen Windows at Jeffreys Bay, South Africa. Surfers also congregate at Sugar Shack, Timmy Turner's family's breakfast spot in Huntington Beach; Zell and Gary Dwelley's Beach Break in Oceanside; and Esau's in Carpinteria near Rincon.

These are the tribal trading posts, where people connect, meet their friends, make new ones, and hear about the ones they've lost contact with. And get a great meal in the bargain.

All ashore in Zihuatanejo.

Avocados Stuffed with Jumbo Shrimp

I first got this easy recipe from Denny Doyle many years ago. It never fails to satisfy.

SERVES 6

1 tablespoon extra-virgin olive oil
6 shell-on jumbo shrimp
A couple of squeezes of fresh lime juice
3 avocados, very ripe but clean and bright green inside

½ cup light mayonnaise
2 tablespoons finely chopped chipotle chiles
Sea salt, to taste

Heat olive oil in a skillet over medium heat and sauté shrimp until just pink, about 3 minutes. Remove from heat, remove shells, and chop coarsely. Refrigerate in a bowl and keep cold in lime juice (the juice keeps the avocado from browning).

When ready to serve, halve avocados, remove pits, score flesh with crisscross cuts, and set aside.

Mix mayonnaise and chiles in a small bowl and spoon mixture into avocado halves. Top with chopped shrimp, and season to taste with lime juice and salt, as needed. Serve immediately on individual plates and eat with a spoon to scoop bites of avocado and shrimp.

PUNTA MITA, NAYARIT
Doña Victoria's Kahlúa Coconut Flan

No dessert is quite as Mexican as flan. Flan is to Mexico what croissants are to France, what apple pie is to the United States.

My head chef at Margarita's Village, Victoria Hernandez, came to us from Guadalajara, but she was born near Punta Mita. This lady, whose regal bearing, immense culinary knowledge, and amazing creations were a joy to experience, gave me a master's class in Mexican cooking.

She had a signature dish that we named Filet Doña Victoria—a prime cut of filet mignon topped with a dark chocolate Oaxacan mole negro. I thought of including it in this book, but the recipe has more than thirty ingredients and takes several hours to make. The next best thing is her flan. It too is a little complicated, but the coconut and Kahlúa makes it so delicious that no other dessert compares. My wife still makes it for special occasions.

SERVES 6

2 cups sugar
½ cup water
5 large eggs
10 ounces whole milk
3 cups condensed milk (preferably Eagle Brand)

1 to 2 ounces Kahlúa, to taste
¾ cup grated fresh coconut
1 cup raspberries
Leaves from 6 sprigs fresh mint

In a small, heavy saucepan over medium-high heat, bring sugar and water to a boil, stirring until sugar dissolves. Let mixture bubble until it is a deep golden color.

Pour into 6 ceramic ramekins, approximately 4 x 2 inches, filling to a depth of about ½ inch, and set aside. Be careful—caramel is very hot!

Preheat oven to 300°F. In a blender, blend eggs, milk, condensed milk, and Kahlúa until smooth. Stir in coconut flakes and carefully pour mixture into ramekins to within ½ inch from top.

Place ramekins in large roasting pan in oven. Carefully add hot water to pan, approximately halfway up sides of ramekins. Reduce heat to 250°F. Bake until flan is set but still wiggly in center, a knife comes out clean, and coconut is golden, 1 to 1½ hours. Remove ramekins from pan; let cool, then cover and transfer to refrigerator to cool completely.

When ready to serve, run a knife around custard edges and tap ramekins at their base to loosen. Invert onto serving plates. If custard does not come out easily, place ramekins briefly in a shallow pan of hot water for 30 seconds to a minute at most.

Garnish with raspberries and mint leaves. Bet your friends they can't take just one bite!

THE CARIBBEAN
A Stream of Tropical Feasts

I spent the better part of a year exploring the Caribbean on the *Indies Trader*, searching for undiscovered waves and organizing trips for marine biologists to map reefs for UCLA's Reefcheck program. It was all sponsored by the Quiksilver Crossing Project, which I directed during that time. I felt lucky to get a dream job once again.

The *Indies Trader* visited every country in the Caribbean basin. Each has its own claim to fame: dance, fashion, music, language, even accents. And, of course, cuisine.

Waves, too, are marked by their particular islands. Great waves certainly exist in the West Indies, but you need the right vessel to find many of them. And while we didn't find surf on every one, the potential was always there for those willing to wait. Patience is vital here, and the local people exercise patience liberally.

Great food, on the other hand, is easy to find—every local market, harbor restaurant, hotel bar, dockside booth, and fishing boat offers up something amazing. So even though you may be occasionally starved for waves, you'll never actually go hungry.

Pat O'Connell, Barbados

In the Caribbean, a boat gets you to the best waves—and often the best food. At St. Barts.

Jerk Chicken Salad 180

Rosemary Sea Scallops with Tamarind Olive Sauce 183

Caribbean Barry's Barracuda 185

Ti Punch Rum Cocktail 186

Santo Domingo Sweet Potatoes with Pineapple Rum Balsamic Glaze 189

Trinidad Coleslaw 190

Bajan Flying Fish 193

Bananas Guadeloupe 197

POTTER'S CAY, NASSAU, BAHAMAS

Harboring Secrets

Harbors are the islands' center of energy. Boats and boating are the major occupation: small rowboats loaded with bait fish, cabin cruisers lounging at sea, schooners rigging their masts, runabouts carrying tourists, trawlers returning with the early catch.

Along the waterfront, fishermen in small skiffs hand off baskets of avocados, papayas, and limes to dark-skinned ladies who sway up the sand, their cargo balanced on their brightly turbaned heads. The clouds edged on the horizon have just a tiny tint of pink dawn left, cotton puffs on a blue tarpaulin of sea. Next to a small stone jetty, four floating market boats anchor, and people crowd on board to buy products from other islands.

Ducking under the booms and stepping over coiled lines, a big schooner's crew unloads its cargo buckets. Its crane swings nets full of live fish onto the dock. On the other side of the wharf, fishermen heave small tubs of shrimp off their boats, briny, mucky, glittering in the sharp sunlight. Along the weathered wharf, carts loaded with conch and clams stutter over the wooden walkway up to the main market area. The secret to good eating in the Caribbean is getting to the market early. You want fresh? This is the place. You want surf? Outer Islands like Eleuthera and the Abacos are a short morning sail. You want paradise? Look around you.

Lunchtime on the Indies Trader

Joel Parkinson making the most of a nice point in St. Barths.

MAKKA BEACH, JAMAICA
One World

There's every kind of wave in the West Indies, just like there's every kind of island—and every kind of cuisine. In an area the size of Texas are twenty-five countries, and each island has its own blend of colonial influences. Many islands are populated with descendants of African slaves, Asian workers from mining and sugar plantation days, Bermudans from India, Cubans from China, Trinidadians from Syria. Even Portuguese and Swedes claimed outposts in this melting pot on the ring of fire. And, of course, there are the cultures that colonized: the French, the British, the Dutch. So when you hear people call it a mixture of cultures, it really is like Bob Marley's "one world"—the globe in a microcosm. The dish below is sure to make everyone *get together and feel all right.*

Jerk Chicken Salad

Jamaica's St. Ann Parish is notable for three things: It's the birthplace of Bob Marley, the site of Jamaica's best wave, and home to one of the finest restaurants on the island. Just around the corner from where Bob Marley was born, Makka Beach is an urchin-covered reef that sometimes gets double-overhead waves with tube sections and big faces for carving turns. Miss T's Kitchen is a color-drenched local eatery in Ocho Rios's funky downtown, serving healthy, home-style Jamaican fare that includes vegan dishes and a mean jerk chicken. Cooked on an open grill with pimento wood chips from the allspice tree—the main spice used for the jerk rub—it is, as Marley might say, *belly full eat good.*

SERVES 6

4 large green onions, white and light green parts only, chopped

1 Maui sweet onion, chopped

2 Scotch bonnet chile peppers, stems removed, chopped fine

½-inch piece fresh ginger, peeled and coarsely chopped

6 cloves garlic, peeled

2 tablespoons soy sauce

2 tablespoons dark brown sugar

¼ cup crumbled fresh thyme

1 tablespoon allspice berries, finely ground

1 tablespoon five-spice powder

1 tablespoon sea salt

1 tablespoon freshly ground black pepper

½ cup canola oil

Juice of 2 limes

1 tablespoon white or apple cider vinegar

Aromatic wood chips for the grill

6 boneless, skin-on chicken thighs

Put everything but the chicken (and wood chips!) in a blender or food processor and purée to make a thick paste. Slather all over chicken, including under the skin. Wrap in plastic wrap or in a large plastic bag and marinate in refrigerator for 3 to 8 hours. Bring to room temperature before cooking.

Light a charcoal grill and bring to medium heat or preheat a gas grill to 350°F. Add 2 large handfuls of aromatic wood chips and close grill. When smoke becomes thick and white, place chicken on grate, skin side up, and cover. Grill until chicken is almost mahogany in color, about 6 minutes. Turn thighs over to skin side and grill for another 4 minutes, watching carefully so the skin doesn't burn. Jerk chicken is done when skin is burnished brown and juices run completely clear. Set aside to rest while you assemble the salad.

SALAD

I prefer butter lettuce for this salad, but feel free to use your favorite. Also note that my good friend Keiko Beatie says that to make it an authentic Bob Marley recipe, you should sprinkle it with 1 teaspoon Jamaican ganja herb. (That's totally — *and recommendably* — optional!)

8 cups lettuce (preferably butter lettuce, but any will work)
2 cups cubed pineapple (½-inch chunks)
2 cups mandarin orange segments
½ cup dried cranberries
½ cup chopped fresh cilantro
6 green onions, sliced
Agave Lime Dressing (*recipe follows*)
2 teaspoons flaxseeds
2 teaspoons sesame seeds

Combine salad greens, pineapple, mandarin orange segments, cranberries, cilantro, and green onion in a large bowl. Divide salad evenly onto 6 plates. Just before serving, drizzle dressing over salad, sprinkle with flax and sesame seeds, and top with warm Jerk Chicken thighs.

AGAVE LIME DRESSING

½ cup sesame oil
¼ cup agave nectar
¼ cup apple cider vinegar
2 tablespoons finely diced onion
2 tablespoons fresh lime juice
1 tablespoon Myers's dark Jamaican rum
Pinch of sea salt, plus more to taste

Place all of the ingredients into a food processor or blender and blend until smooth. Taste and add more salt if needed. Store in a lidded jar in the refrigerator until needed.

PINE CAY, TURKS & CAICOS
Enjoying the Cordon Blues

One of the pleasant surprises about crewing on the *Indies Trader* was the food. While the cabins were small and the accommodations spartan, eating was an unanticipated extravagance. Every cook who served on the boat had been trained at a top culinary institute. The truth was, these guys could have been employed in any of the world's finest restaurants. But their passion for surfing and their love of the sailing life had brought them here instead, where places like Pine Cay gave them the best of both worlds—much to the benefit of those of us on board. Their menus and presentations were four-star affairs, all the more impressive when produced from a galley the size of a closet. I learned a lot from them about tight-space kitchen techniques as well as about creating gourmet meals from whatever fish, meat, and produce was available at the local marketplace.

Rosemary Sea Scallops
with Tamarind Olive Sauce

SERVES 6, as an appetizer

¼ cup fresh lime juice

¼ cup extra-virgin olive oil

¼ cup Royal Oak Trinidad rum

½ teaspoon Turks & Caicos sea salt

18 large diver scallops

6 rosemary branches (about 8 inches long)

1 red bell pepper, cut into 18 (1-inch) squares

Tamarind Olive Sauce (*recipe follows*)

Mix lime juice, olive oil, rum, and salt in a bowl. Add scallops, mix well, and marinate in refrigerator for at least 30 minutes. Remove scallops from marinade and set both aside.

Light a charcoal grill and bring to medium-high heat or preheat a gas grill to 350° to 400°F.

To make the skewers, strip needles off rosemary branches, leaving last 2 inches of needles. Soak rosemary branches in cold water for a few minutes, and then thread 3 marinated scallops and 3 red bell pepper squares on each skewer.

Grill skewers until scallops are no longer translucent, brushing with remaining marinade, just 1 to 2 minutes per side. Transfer to a platter and spoon Tamarind Olive Sauce over skewers, or divide scallops onto 6 dinner plates and pass sauce separately for dipping.

TAMARIND OLIVE SAUCE

⅓ cup tamarind pulp, seeded

¼ cup sour cream

¼ cup mayonnaise

¼ cup finely chopped green olives

¼ cup finely chopped black Kalamata olives

In a medium bowl, combine all ingredients together and mix well. Sauce can be made in advance and stored in the refrigerator; bring to room temperature before serving.

MOUNT IRVINE BAY, TOBAGO
Barry's World

Spending months in a location instead of just days lets a traveler ease in and get tuned in. A ten-month stay is not just a taste of the culture; it's a rich, satisfying meal. In Tobago, where one of the world's great waves slumbers secretly in plain sight, surfer Barry St. George runs a diving enterprise. Knowing he was one of the key chieftains in Tobago's surf kingdom, I invited him to come on the *Indies Trader* for a few days before we pulled into port. We sailed to places on his own island he hadn't surfed before. From then on we were everyone's friend. And we surfed on perfect days when that legendary roping wave was winding across a reef the length of a football field.

One afternoon, Barry went out and speared a fish. On the way home, we stopped to pick various fruits right off trees. That night we had a big *barbacoa* and cooked over an open grill. In the garden we grabbed a few tomatoes and summer squash. We had a millionaire's feast and never even went to a store. You can live in a thatched-roof cottage and feel like a rich man in Tobago.

Caribbean Barry's Barracuda

Here's the closest facsimile of the recipe for the barracuda we had that night in Tobago. Use whatever good citrus and/or tropical fruits you can get your hands on. Also note that you can serve the fruit on top of the fish, or arrange the fish on a bed of the fruit—it's all good. This preparation is a winner with many other kinds of fish, too: swordfish steaks, grilled rare ahi, any fish you find extremely fresh at the seafood market.

SERVES 6

¼ cup white wine vinegar

¼ cup fruity extra-virgin olive oil

¼ cup fresh orange juice

3 tablespoons soy sauce

2 tablespoons grated parmesan cheese

1 tablespoon Italian spices (mixed oregano, rosemary, basil, thyme, marjoram, sage, or garlic powder)

¼ cup minced fresh garlic, divided

2½-pound piece of barracuda or ahi

1 white guava, peeled and chopped, or ½ cup chopped pineapple

Fruit from 1 yellow passionfruit, or 2 or 3 chopped kiwis

½ cup small orange sections

½ cup chopped papaya

½ cup pink grapefruit sections

2 tablespoons minced ginger

Prepare the fish: In a medium bowl, stir together vinegar, olive oil, orange juice, soy sauce, parmesan, Italian spices, and most of the garlic, reserving a couple of teaspoons of garlic for later. Pour mixture over fish in a glass bowl or freezer bag. Marinate in refrigerator for 15 to 20 minutes at most, turning once.

Light a charcoal grill and bring to medium-low to medium heat or preheat a gas grill to 300°F to 350°F. While the grill is warming up, sauté reserved garlic in a small pan for 1 to 2 minutes, until fragrant.

Once the grill is hot, cook marinated fish on grill to sear the outside; inside of fish should be rare.

While the fish cooks, combine guava, passionfruit, orange, papaya, grapefruit, and ginger in a medium bowl and mix well. Arrange fruit on a serving platter.

When the fish is done, slice into 6 fillets, arrange atop the fruit, and sprinkle with sautéed minced garlic. Alternatively, you can put the fish on the platter first and top with the fruit.

JOST VAN DYKE, BRITISH VIRGIN ISLANDS
Foxy's Bar

Foxy's Bar is the place to be on New Year's Eve—or as Foxy calls it, "Old Year's Night." The little island of Jost Van Dyke in the British Virgin Islands is a magnet for fun lovers year-round, but December 31 is definitely the highlight.

It's just a short hop from St. Thomas, where we'd spent the last week of 2003 scoring good waves. We decided to check out the party that in previous years had attracted the Rolling Stones, Kate Moss, Tom Cruise, and the Beach Boys. As we sailed the *Indies Trader* into Great Harbor on Jost Van Dyke, our vessel's tattoo-style paint job and pirate-ship flair was an instant hit with the hundreds of vessels anchored throughout the cay. On our way toward the beach in our little tin boat, we must have accepted invitations from a dozen yachts, each offering an array of gourmet food and exotic drinks. By the time we actually landed and staggered into Foxy's, we were already—to use the strict nautical term—three sheets to the wind.

Ti Punch Rum Cocktail

Ti punch, Martinique's national cocktail, has the same ingredients as the gin gimlet, which is now enjoying a huge (and well-deserved) revival. Pronounced "tee paunch" in the Caribbean—"*ti*" being Creole slang for the French *petit*—it's one of the most underrated and authentic Caribbean cocktails.

MAKES 1 COCKTAIL

1 ounce cane syrup (or substitute simple syrup or a teaspoon of sugar)
1 lime wedge (the juicier the better)

2 ounces Martinique *rhum agricole,* light or dark (preferably Clément Blanc, but any good rum will do)
Strip of lime and/or orange peel

Splash cane syrup and a big squeeze of lime over a glass of ice and add rum. Gently stir and garnish with lime and/or orange peel.

Barbados locals at home

TOINY COAST, ST. BARTS

Don't Fly Her Till You See the Whites of Their Eyes

St. Bartholomew Island's old stone port was built in the 1500s and still looks much the same—like a *Pirates of the Caribbean* set. It's a safe, friendly, mellow island, with some occasionally great waves and fabulous food from the French. The airport, however, is far from mellow—or seemingly safe.

On my first flight to St. Barts, I was the only passenger in a four-seater Piper Cherokee. The airport is on one side and the harbor is on the other, split by a high ridge. It was a relatively windy day during hurricane season, and the flight path goes right over the crest. The pilot actually had me hold down a lever from the ceiling of the cockpit, which I assume was a stabilizing gear. I don't know how close an aircraft is supposed to get to a ridgeline, but I remember seeing the cigarette in the driver's mouth as a car passed below us. They say you're too close when you can see the whites of their eyes. I saw his, and my own whites were huge at that moment.

Later that night, John, the gracious owner of the St. Barts Quiksilver store, and his lovely French wife settled me right down with a couple of glasses of stiff ti punch and this delicious dish.

The landing strip at St. Barts

Santo Domingo Sweet Potatoes with Pineapple Rum Balsamic Glaze

This is a fine companion to grilled or roasted fish or pork, or all on its own for a vegetarian main dish.

SERVES 6

6 cups peeled, cubed boniato (white) sweet potatoes

1 cup thinly sliced Maui sweet onion

¼ cup extra-virgin olive oil

1½ cups chunked pineapple

1 tablespoon freshly grated ginger

½ teaspoon finely chopped fresh rosemary

1 teaspoon Turks & Caicos sea salt

¼ teaspoon freshly ground black pepper

¼ cup balsamic vinegar glaze

½ cup Caribbean molasses

¼ cup Mount Gay Barbados rum, divided

Preheat oven to 450°F. Place sweet potatoes and onion in a plastic freezer bag, then drizzle olive oil over. Toss to coat completely, seal tightly, and let marinate for 20 minutes.

Cover a baking sheet with aluminum foil and lay out the potatoes, onions, and pineapple chunks in a single layer, sprinkling evenly with ginger, rosemary, salt, and pepper. Use two sheets if needed, but make sure they fit on same rack in oven.

Place baking sheet in oven and roast until potatoes start to brown, about 30 minutes. Remove from oven, turn all items over, and drizzle balsamic glaze, molasses, and half the rum on each sweet potato (the molasses and rum will help caramelize the glaze). Return to oven and roast another 20 minutes.

When the potato mixture is browned to your liking, remove from oven and splash remaining rum over all ingredients. Use a spatula to gently transfer sweet potato mixture to a platter or bowl, and serve as a side with flying fish or pork.

AIRPORTS, TOBAGO
Trinidad Coleslaw

The Caribbean is about color: skin tones from coffee to cream, ocean shades from emerald to indigo, foods in vivid primary hues. Underwater are red parrot fish, silver barracuda, orange starfish, and purple urchins. Colors celebrate the tastes of the Caribbean too: sweet, tart, piquant, aromatic, and citrus. This classic Trinidad coleslaw is the color of the Caribbean. And the taste of rapture.

This is delicious with jerk chicken; see the recipe for it on page 181. Make sure to put some Burning Spear tunes on while you enjoy this.

SERVES 6

5 cups shredded white cabbage

1 cup shredded purple cabbage

2 to 3 carrots, sliced into 2-inch matchsticks (about 1 cup)

1 cup cubed pineapple (½-inch chunks)

½ large red bell pepper, cut into ¼-inch x 1-inch pieces

3 spring onions, cut into ¼-inch x ½-inch pieces

3 green onions, diced

Trinidad Dressing (*recipe follows*)

¼ cup minced parsley

3 tablespoons sunflower seeds

Combine both types of cabbage, carrots, pineapple, bell pepper, spring onion, and green onions in a bowl. Mix in dressing and toss to evenly coat slaw completely.

Sprinkle with parsley and sunflower seeds, and serve.

TRINIDAD DRESSING

¼ cup honey

2 tablespoons extra-virgin olive oil

2 tablespoons fresh lemon juice

1 tablespoon Dijon mustard

1 tablespoon Kraken Black Spiced rum

1 tablespoon light mayonnaise

½ Scotch bonnet chile pepper, seeds removed, minced (about 1 tablespoon)

1 teaspoon Antilles Spice Clipper passionfruit hot sauce, or your choice hot sauce (optional)

1 teaspoon minced garlic

1 teaspoon Turks & Caicos sea salt

¼ teaspoon white pepper

Combine all the dressing ingredients in a jar or bowl: honey, olive oil, lemon juice, mustard, rum, mayonnaise, chile pepper (and hot sauce, if using), garlic, salt, and white pepper. Set aside.

CABARETE, DOMINICAN REPUBLIC
The Red Hot Chile Peppers

Columbus never reached the spice islands of India—he ran into the Caribbean on the way. But he found a spice that ended up having more of an effect on world cuisine than almost any other: peppers. Columbus's home base was Dominica, now officially the Commonwealth of Dominica, where Spain opened a trade in chile peppers with countries all over the globe, starting a gastronomy of heat. Until the Spaniards introduced the capsicum family of plants to Europe and beyond, there were no Italian hot sausages, Indian chicken vindaloo, Sichuan kung pao chicken, Portuguese peri-peri shrimp, Thai green curry, Korean kimchi, or Moroccan harissa. The red hot chile peppers brought back from the New World revolutionized cooking across the planet and created whole new regional cuisines—based around the pepper—that *never existed before*.

Think what Hunan, Madras, Peruvian, Javanese, and Sonoran cooking would be like if there were no chiles involved. Until those capsicums came crashing into our respective cuisines, it was a pretty bland world.

SOUP BOWLS, BARBADOS
Kelly's Second Mom

Ann Thompson is the head chieftess of Barbados when it comes to all things surf. She and her husband, Bill, started the Lazy Days Surf Shop in 1978, and ever since she's been supporting surf contests, making friends, doing good deeds, and putting up wayward surfers.

One of her early wayward sons was Kelly Slater, the world's best-known surf icon. She's been a substitute mother hen for Kelly (and the rest of us) for several decades now, introducing him and us to Soup Bowls, the island's premier surf spot. Kelly, who calls it one of his top three waves in the world, cut his teeth here on the heavy reef break before venturing to Hawaii.

Irrepressible, incorrigible, and hilariously delightful, Ann personifies the Bajan love of community. And her family's humble generosity knows no bounds.

When I left Barbados after a lengthy stay, she gave me a cookbook by her friend Dunstan Harris called *Island Cooking.* In Queen Ann's honor, here's a recipe from it.

Homemade Caribbean Seasoning

Sure, you can buy Mrs. Dash Caribbean Citrus seasoning, or you can have the fun of making it yourself. My preferred blend is based on what I've had in the Caribbean. Combine 1 teaspoon each of sea salt, onion powder, dried thyme, garlic powder, ground coriander, ground turmeric, black pepper, dried parsley, marjoram, powdered ginger, fenugreek powder, and ground cumin. Add ½ teaspoon each anise powder, allspice, cinnamon, dried mustard, mace, and ground cardamom, along with a pinch of minced habanero and a pinch of powdered makrut lime. Store in a jar in a dry place.

Ross Williams stirring it up at Soup Bowls

Bajan Flying Fish

Barbados is sometimes called the "land of the flying fish," because these beautiful fish actually glide through the air for twenty feet or more at up to thirty miles an hour, spreading their pectoral fins like birds in flight. They make delicious eating. It's the national dish of Barbados for a reason.

SERVES 4

⅓ cup fresh lime juice (about 2 limes)

¾ cup water

4 flying fish fillets (or substitute small snapper)

2 large eggs

2 tablespoons Mrs. Dash Caribbean Citrus Seasoning Blend

1 cup all-purpose flour

1 cup Italian-style breadcrumbs

1 teaspoon paprika

1 small Scotch bonnet chile, seeds removed and cut in ½-inch slivers

1 tablespoon Emeril Lagasse Cajun Seasoning Blend (optional)

½ teaspoon sea salt

½ teaspoon white pepper

Canola oil, for frying

3 cloves garlic, minced

6 cups fresh spinach, washed

1 cup cherry tomatoes, halved

Squeeze limes into a bowl with water and add fish to soak for 30 minutes. Remove fish, rinse, and pat dry.

In a small bowl, whisk together eggs and Caribbean seasoning. Set aside.

In another bowl, stir together flour, breadcrumbs, paprika, Scotch bonnet chile, Cajun seasoning (if using), salt, and white pepper.

Coat the bottom of a large frying pan generously with oil and place over medium-high heat. Dip fish into egg mixture, shaking off any excess egg. Coat each fillet in breadcrumb mixture, shake again, and carefully place skin side up in oil. Fry for no more than 2 minutes per side; fish in hot oil cooks very fast, so be careful not to overcook. Remove from oil, drain on paper towels, and place on a warm platter while you cook the spinach.

In another large skillet, heat 1 tablespoon oil over medium-low heat. Add garlic and sauté for 1 minute, until aromatic. Toss in spinach, quickly tossing for 10 seconds, until just barely wilted, then transfer to a serving platter. Arrange fish atop spinach, top with cherry tomatoes, and serve.

Next pages: Bathsheba, in Barbados. Check out the mushroom rocks, the pines, and palms that grow right down to the water's edge.

GUADELOUPE HARBOR, LESSER ANTILLES
Market Day

The typical Caribbean market springs up each Saturday morning like a movie set: a tent city of umbrellas, stalls, and booths with straw hats and bright floral fabrics tucked among rows of food stalls piled with pyramids of fruit. Steel drum bands and troubadours wedge between aisles of fishmongers, butchers, and produce hawkers. Best of all are the mobile grill carts selling freshly baked pineapple toast, guava bread, and steaming Bahamian-style grits with stewed fish.

Early shoppers (mostly from restaurants and food stores) hunt for bargains or hustle to get "first pick" quality. Ben, the *Indies Trader* chef, would dart from stall to stall, searching for the items on his shopping list. I often took a more leisurely pace, comparing the seafood on offer to that from neighboring islands and studying the unique local produce. We'd be done shopping by 7:30 a.m. On the way back to the *Indies Trader*, we'd check to see if the swell had come up. If it had, we'd unload the provisions in the galley, jump in the water, and get in a good session before the wind came up.

We visited a multitude of Caribbean markets: Cheapside Public Market in Barbados, Mercado Modelo in Santo Domingo, Chaguanas Market in Trinidad, Potter's Cay in Nassau, and the floating market in Curaçao. But nothing matched the size, color, and variety of Guadeloupe harbor's open-air Pointe-à-Pitre market: big, bright umbrella stands piled with plaid sacks of spices; bananas in thirty-pound bunches; crates of fresh mangoes; Martinique rum...it's Timbuktu meets old Honolulu by way of Amsterdam.

Market day in St George's, Grenadines

Bananas Guadeloupe

SERVES 6

3 tablespoons butter
3 bananas, cut in half lengthwise
Handful of raisins
1½ teaspoons vanilla extract

3 spears fresh pineapple, crushed
 (about ¾ cup)
2 tablespoons frozen orange juice concentrate
3 tablespoons rum

Melt butter in a skillet over medium-low heat. Add bananas and cook until browned. Turn over and brown the other side. Remove bananas and set on serving plate. Add raisins, vanilla, pineapple, orange juice concentrate, and rum to warm skillet. Stir to combine and cook until heated through and raisins are plumped. Spoon warm sauce over bananas and serve.

INDONESIA
Grilling in the Ring of Fire

KUTA BEACH, BALI

My love affair with Indonesia started early. Having visited Indo with my parents as a kid, I saw the early surf discoverers at Kuta Beach in Bali and wanted to return as soon as I could to try those waves myself. I've managed to get back a few times, and it's always been both a surfing and an eating highlight.

Despite the teeming cities in the world's fourth-largest nation, Indonesia's surfing areas enjoy an indolent atmosphere—languid, relaxed, hospitable—that is mostly unaffected by the hectic metropolises and ever-present chance of political upheaval, deadly epidemic, earthquake, volcanic eruption, and tsunami. In Indonesia's volcanic ring of fire, mythical waves have been the talk of surfing explorers since the 1960s. Exploring the more than 17,000 islands by boat and jungle trails over the last three decades has revealed a rich wave field that is unequaled in any of the world's other island chains. Swells parade across the Indian Ocean, arching and undulating like the backs of dancing cobras before striking hard on the coral reefs.

As for the food, Indonesia is an exotic cultural soup. The Malays, Dutch, Indians, Portuguese, Middle Easterners, and of course Indonesians have all contributed to this thriving culinary cacophony. With more than 5,000 traditional recipes, Indonesia's culinary range is as astonishing in depth and variety as its waves.

A hotel entrance in Bali

At higher tide a wave breaks right across these outside rocks in Plengkung, Grajagan Bay (G-land)

Rice Paper Summer Rolls with Soy-Glazed Pork   203

Balinese Beef Satay   206

Rujak   209
Spicy-Sweet Fruit Salad

Terung Lodeh   210
Spicy-Sweet Shrimp & Eggplant Soup

Pepes Ikan   214
Steamed Chile Ginger Halibut

Gado Gado   216
Blanched Vegetables in Peanut Sauce

PLENGKUNG, GRAJAGAN BAY (G-LAND)

G-Land: Where the Ancient Forest Emerged from the Sea

In 1974, when Pipeline master Gerry Lopez, Peter McCabe, and a handful of friends beached their skiffs at Grajagan Bay, they didn't know they were following in the footsteps of the European explorers who'd discovered this archipelago exactly 460 years earlier. They'd brought provisions and surfboards—which was more than intrepid adventurers Bill Boyum and Bob Laverty had when they came upon the wave breaking along the jungle-covered Alas Purwo National Park two years earlier. Marooned on this stretch of coast one night, Boyum and Laverty awoke the following morning to see one of the world's supreme lineups.

In the Kejawen religious tradition (a Javanese blend of animistic, Buddhist, Hindu, and Sufi Muslim beliefs), Grajagan is considered the exact spot where the earth first emerged from the ocean and became Alas Purwo—the ancient forest. This later became the exact spot where intrepid wave exploration transformed into a new form of surf travel: the surf resort.

Bob Boyum, Bill's younger brother, was the creative genius behind this idea. While Lopez and McCabe explored the limits of long, deep tube riding, the Boyums started the first surf camps, which are now found at nearly every remote surf spot on the planet. Soon our staff at *Surfer* was documenting both the feats of high performance and the embryonic cottage industry of surf cottages.

The Dutch traders in the age of discovery managed to hold onto their Indonesian colony for more than four centuries, but other than their culinary contribution, they have little remaining influence on the place today. The Boyums, who built their mystical surf camp in lofty tree houses to protect guests from tigers, tsunamis, and sweltering heat, were able to hold onto their prized possession for only a few years. But their contribution to surfing's age of discovery and Indonesian surf lore left a legacy arguably as influential as that of the colonials.

Pure gold at G-Land

LAGUNDRI BAY, NIAS
Running Amok

The phrase "run amok" has Malay-Indonesian roots. "Amok" came from the Indonesian word *mengamuk,* which roughly translates as "to make a furious and desperate charge." It comes from a spiritual belief that amok is caused by *hantu belian,* an evil tiger spirit that enters a body and causes the person to commit heinous acts. Because of this belief, Indonesians would try to tolerate and deal with bad behavior without bearing ill will toward the person who was behaving badly. (See the outdoor room with a view on the next page.)

Here's a story of when ocean spirits ran amok. Surfers Richard Marsh, John Philbin, and Richie Lovett were at G-Land when the devastating 1994 tsunami hit. "When the roar grew louder, I sat up inside my mosquito net," said John, "and just as I did, a churning wall of water blew through my hut." Richie described the experience as "being hit by a train at full speed." Richard Marsh thought he was being attacked by a tiger until he realized it was a wave. John found protection, but Richard and Richie were swept hundreds of feet into the jungle by the wave.

"I was completely panicking," said Richard. "It was a matter of surviving, just grabbing onto things to stay above the water, trying to keep all the debris away from my head and, above all, to get a breath. The hut had disappeared, and I was entwined in logs and trees and bits of bamboo. When the water started to subside, I was stuck with my legs pinned under a whole lot of logs and rubbish."

Boating amok

Rice Paper Summer Rolls with Soy-Glazed Pork

A dish shaped like a log is appropriate for the running-amok story, don't you think? This recipe comes from the little restaurant that used to sit on the bay at Nias, where an almost-perfect wave reeled past a palm-fringed backdrop straight out of a *King Kong* film. Destroyed during the same tsunami, it was replaced by a new establishment that is far cleaner and has great food. The wave has come back, too.

They make these summer rolls vegetarian, and so can you if you omit the pork or substitute tofu cubes. Just don't attempt to eat them during a tsunami.

Note: Kecap manis (Indonesian sweet soy sauce) is easy to make yourself. Just boil together ¼ cup soy sauce and ⅜ cup brown sugar, then let it cool and thicken.

SERVES 6 (makes 18 rice paper rolls)

2 tablespoons kecap manis

4 tablespoons soy sauce, divided

3 tablespoons honey

2 tablespoons oyster sauce

2 pounds pork shoulder

2 tablespoons light sesame oil

2 large carrots, cut into matchsticks

1 small red bell pepper, cut into matchsticks

1 cup thinly shredded Chinese cabbage

1 cup roughly chopped fresh mint leaves

¾ cup roughly chopped fresh cilantro

1 tablespoon sweet chile sauce

18 rice paper rounds (or 36 if double-wrapping the rolls)

1 cup bean sprouts

In a large bowl, combine kecap manis, 2 tablespoons soy sauce, honey, and oyster sauce. Mix until smooth, then transfer 1 or 2 tablespoons of sauce to a small bowl for later use. Fully coat pork with remaining sauce. Cover and marinate for at least 30 minutes or up to overnight in refrigerator.

When ready to cook, preheat oven to 350°F. Light a charcoal grill and bring to medium-high heat or preheat a gas grill to 350°F to 400°F. Remove pork from marinade, reserving marinade. Grill for 2 to 3 minutes on each side, browning well. Transfer to a medium roasting pan and baste with reserved marinade. Place in oven and roast for 3 hours. While pork is roasting, heat sesame oil in a medium skillet over medium-high heat and stir-fry carrots, bell pepper, and cabbage for 1 minute. Transfer to a work surface. Combine mint and cilantro in a small bowl and set aside.

When pork is falling-apart tender, remove from oven. Cool for 30 minutes and shred finely. Spoon several tablespoons of remaining sauce over pork and mix well. Combine remaining 2 tablespoons soy sauce and sweet chile sauce in a small bowl and set aside. Fill a large bowl with hot water. With a pair of wood tongs, carefully dip a round of rice paper into water until soft. Lay on flat work surface. Place 2 tablespoons each of pork mixture and vegetables onto rice paper. Add large pinch of bean sprouts and sprinkle with some mint-cilantro mixture. Fold up two ends of rice paper, then wrap a side over filling and roll tight like a burrito. Repeat until all rolls are made. Serve with sweet chile sauce/soy sauce mixture.

*A Balinese mask that perfectly
illustrates "running amok"*

*A beachside view at Nias when
the ocean wasn't running amok*

Balinese Beef Satay

While beef satay can be found in food carts and *warungs* (small restaurants or cafés) from Nias to New Guinea, it is also a very practical food for camping—you can cook it quickly over an open fire or a grill.

Note: Fish sauce is widely available in the Asian section of supermarkets; any kind will work. If you put the beef in the freezer for a while to firm it up before slicing, it'll cut much more easily.

SERVES 6

¼ cup packed brown sugar

¼ cup fish sauce

2 tablespoons minced onion

2 green onions, diced

4 cloves garlic, crushed

1 tablespoon freshly grated ginger

2 tablespoons dark sesame oil

2 tablespoons soy sauce

2 tablespoons ground coriander

1 tablespoon ground cumin

½ teaspoon ground turmeric

⅛ teaspoon cayenne pepper

2-inch piece of fresh lemongrass (white part only, minced)

2½ pounds beef top sirloin, trimmed and cut into 14 to 18 strips about 3 inches long and ⅛-inch thick

12 (10-inch) wooden skewers, soaked in water for 30 minutes

Sea salt, to taste

6 tablespoons creamy peanut butter thinned with 2 tablespoons milk

1 cucumber, sliced

Sweet Chile Sauce (*see recipe page 214*)

In a large bowl, combine brown sugar, fish sauce, onion, green onions, garlic, ginger, sesame oil, soy sauce, coriander, cumin, turmeric, and cayenne pepper. Stir together until smooth. Stir in minced lemongrass. Toss beef in marinade until thoroughly coated. Cover with plastic wrap and marinate in refrigerator for at least 2 hours or up to overnight. When ready to grill, remove beef from the fridge for about 30 minutes so it comes to room temperature.

Light a charcoal grill and bring to high heat or preheat a gas grill to 425° to 450°F. Oil grill grate lightly with a basting brush.

Remove beef from marinade and shake off any excess marinade. Thread meat onto skewers and place directly on hot grill, cooking until meat lifts easily from grill, 1 to 2 minutes.

Flip skewers over and cook other side, until meat is lightly charred, about 2 minutes. Return to first side again; grill until meat is cooked through but still slightly pink, about 2 more minutes. Transfer meat to a platter and let rest about 2 more minutes. Taste and add salt if needed.

Serve with thinned peanut butter sauce, cold cucumber slices, and Sweet Chile Sauce.

ULUWATU, BALI
The Surfer's Playground

Characterized by a deep oceanic trench, several marginal basins, thousands of reefs, and an inner curve of extensive volcanic activity, Indonesia is a rich, varied wave field. The Indian Ocean sends massive swells sweeping across the archipelago from the Mentwai Islands near Asia's Malaysian Peninsula to Timor, just a few hundred miles off the northwestern coast of Australia.

Along with waves of every stripe, these islands are home to 300 million ethnically mixed people and some of the planet's most diverse flora, fauna, and topography. Mostly jungle and rain forest, Indonesia has 34,000 miles of coastline, the second largest in the world. This triangulation—a vast, swell-laden ocean; a jumbled, jigsaw-puzzle coastline; and a verdant, tropical climate—is a rare combination indeed. For surfers it is the world's most immense wave playground, with hundreds of perfect setups, constant swells, and warm water.

In particular, Bali, whose gentle people and elegant culture host some of the globe's most famous surf spots, has become the epicenter of Indonesian surfing. It's home to an international cadre of board builders, shop owners, camp hosts, and restaurateurs, all catering to the surf audience.

Market time in Bali

Rujak
Spicy-Sweet Fruit Salad

SERVES 6

1 tart green apple

1 nectarine, ripe and juicy

1 pear, ripe and juicy

1 mandarin orange, peeled

1 mango, peeled and pit removed

2 cups cubed pineapple (1-inch chunks)

1 small cucumber, diced (about 1 cup)

1 jicama, peeled and sliced into ¼-inch sticks

Pinch of tablespoon shrimp paste (*trassi*)

2 tablespoons lemon juice

2 tablespoons water

1 tablespoon soy sauce

1 red chile, minced

¼ cup palm or dark brown sugar

¼ cup coarsely chopped roasted peanuts

Slice up all fruit, leaving skin on apple, nectarine, and pear for health and color. Place with cucumber and jicama in a large salad bowl and set aside.

Wrap shrimp paste in a piece of aluminum foil and roast over grill or in the oven for about 5 minutes. Whisk roasted paste with lemon juice, water, soy sauce, chile, and sugar into a smooth mixture for dressing.

Pour dressing over fruit and toss to mix well. Stir in chopped peanuts. Let salad sit for a few minutes before serving, so flavors combine.

MACARONIS, PULAU PAGAI
Discovering a Gold Field of Waves

The discovery of the Mentawai island chain in the northern Indian Ocean was a turning point in surf history. While working on a salvage boat, Australian surfer Martin Daley noticed an unusual number of wrecks strewn across this almost-unknown archipelago. The reason? Late-night swells would surprise unsuspecting sailing ships anchored on the reefs. When coupled with a falling tide, a strong swell could strand a boat on a reef with a broken back. Martin quickly deduced the potential upside: a multitude of excellent surf breaks.

A born adventurer, entrepreneur, and maverick, Martin was inspired by Ernest Shackleton and his epic explorations in Antarctica. Dreaming big, Martin eventually bought the boat he'd once crewed on and spent a few years with friends working salvage and surfing these islands. The crew took a blood oath to keep their surf spots secret.

Then in 1992, Martin took two-time world champ Tom Carroll and big-wave legend Ross Clarke-Jones to Mentawai, where they scored an epic session of surf. The cat leaped out of the bag. Photos surfaced in magazines, and Martin had more requests from surfers—offering far more money than he could ever make toiling in the salvage business. This led to a whole new chapter in surf travel: the charter-boat surf trip. Bruce Raymond, an ex–professional surfer who was then an executive of Quiksilver Australia, came up with a visionary concept: travel the world looking for undiscovered waves. He hired Martin to captain the vessel, and the Crossing Project was born. Surf travel would never be the same.

Later, Bruce hired me to organize the trips and visitors as the director of the Crossing Project. That meant surf, travel, and global culinary adventures. Once again I'd scored the job of my dreams.

Terung Lodeh
Spicy-Sweet Shrimp & Eggplant Soup

One thing the Crossing Project never lacked was great food. Chefs used both locally sourced ingredients and foods they'd brought from previous legs of the journey, which had started in Indonesia. This spectacular Javanese soup holds its own among the great soups of the world.

SERVES 6

BROTH

1½ tablespoons peanut oil

1 white onion, sliced

1 cup minced mushrooms

¼ cup slivered garlic

¼ cup very thinly sliced fresh ginger

2 cups chicken stock

1 cup water

2 tablespoons soy sauce

½ cup sweet white wine

4 green onions, sliced

2 tablespoons chopped fresh cilantro

1 tablespoon chile sauce

SHRIMP AND EGGPLANT

2 long purple (Chinese) eggplants, quartered
  and cut into 3-inch sticks

Sea salt, to taste

6 tablespoons peanut oil, divided

30 medium shrimp, peeled and deveined

1 small white onion, quartered

12 cherry tomatoes, halved

2 cloves garlic, minced

4 red chiles, sliced

¼ cup coconut cream

1 cup water

2 tablespoons soy sauce

Heat oil in a deep pot over high heat. Stir-fry sliced onions for 3 minutes, until golden. Add mushrooms and cook for 3 minutes, then add garlic and cook for a minute more. Stirring constantly, mix in ginger, then gradually pour in chicken stock, water, and soy sauce.

Add wine, green onions, cilantro, and chile sauce, continuing to stir, then let simmer on very low heat while you prepare the shrimp and eggplant.

Sprinkle eggplant with a pinch of salt. Heat ¼ cup oil in a large skillet over medium heat and add eggplant. Cook, stirring, until browned on all sides, about 5 minutes. Remove from pan and drain.

In the same skillet, sauté shrimp over medium-high heat with 1 tablespoon oil until half cooked, about 2 minutes. Remove and set aside.

In the same skillet, sauté onion over medium-high heat with remaining 1 tablespoon oil until golden, about 4 minutes. Add cherry tomatoes and garlic, and cook for 1 minute more. Mix in chiles, coconut cream, and water, bringing mixture to a boil. Heat until the oil in the coconut cream separates, 3 to 4 minutes.

Reduce heat to a simmer and add soy sauce. Taste and add more salt if needed. Transfer shrimp and eggplant mixture to simmering broth and stir. Cook until flavors are blended, about 5 minutes. Remove from heat and serve in shallow bowls.

PASTA POINT, NORTH MALE ATOLL, MALDIVES
Smashing Plates & Blowing Lids Off

In 2004, a 9.3-magnitude earthquake centered near the west coast of Sumatra generated a tsunami that killed more than 227,000 people. The quake had the energy of 1,500 Hiroshima atomic bombs. Let that sink in for a moment.

The Indonesian archipelago is an arc of more than 100 active volcanoes, gurgling throats of molten lava percolating with the threat of detonation. More than 400 others lie buried in slumbering, malevolent silence. And indeed, in the last decade or so, several more of these furies have blown their tops.

The region is the fracture point between two major tectonic plates. Crunching up like gigantic slices of toast, they eventually shattered into 17,000 islands strewn across a seismic belt of volcanic turmoil. Scientists say this region is a hot spot of the earth's ring of fire, a ring that goes up through the Philippines, Japan, the Aleutians, and down the entire west coast of North, Central, and South America. This ring of fire accounts for ninety percent of the world's earthquakes and volcanic eruptions. The ring is rich with great surf spots and great cuisines—but they could all blow up at any minute.

Put another shrimp on the barbie.

A Rejang dance ritual from the Klungkung district of Bali

An outdoor room with a view at Pasta Point in the Maldives

Pepes Ikan
Steamed Chile Ginger Halibut

The chile sauce in this recipe not only works well with the halibut, but it's perfect to serve with summer rolls and any dish that benefits from a spicy-sweet flavor boost.

SERVES 6

6 halibut fillets (5 ounces each, about 2 pounds)

3-inch-long piece fresh ginger, peeled and slivered

2 cloves garlic, minced

2 tablespoons finely chopped Indonesian
   chile peppers

¼ cup chopped fresh cilantro

5 green onions, cut into 1½-inch-long slices

3 tablespoons fresh lime juice

¼ cup Sweet Chile Sauce (*recipe follows*)

3 lemons, quartered

Line a bamboo steamer (or any steamer basket) with parchment paper or banana leaves, if available. Bring water in steamer to a boil, place fillets in steamer, and sprinkle ginger, garlic, chiles, and cilantro over fish. Cover and steam for 5 to 6 minutes.

Remove lid and sprinkle green onions and lime juice equally over each fillet. Put lid back on steamer until juice is absorbed, about another 30 seconds. Transfer fish to a platter and spoon 2 tablespoons Sweet Chile Sauce over each fillet. Serve with lemon wedges over a bed of jasmine rice.

SWEET CHILE SAUCE

1 cup cane sugar

1 cup water

½ cup rice vinegar

3 to 4 small red chiles, minced, and/or
   2 tablespoons red pepper flakes

3 cloves garlic, slivered

2 tablespoons ruby red sherry

1 tablespoon soy sauce

1 teaspoon ketchup

1½ tablespoons cornstarch

2 tablespoons cold water

Stir sugar into water until dissolved. Combine sugar/water mixture and rice vinegar, chiles, garlic, sherry, soy sauce, and ketchup in a saucepan and bring to a boil, boiling for about 10 minutes.

Mix cornstarch and cold water together in a separate bowl, then slowly add it to saucepan, stirring to mix thoroughly. Continue stirring until sauce thickens, 2 to 4 minutes. Let cool and taste: sweet should be first, then sour, ending with salty. Adjust for sweetness by adding sugar, or for spiciness by adding chiles. Pour into a small jar or bottle with a sealable lid and store in the refrigerator.

LAMNO, SUMATRA

The World's Most Expensive Beverage

Food and drink in Indo take some strange twists. Thanks to the Asian palm civet, a wild, cat-size animal known as a toddy cat, the coffee beans they eat have become the planet's priciest. These small, stocky mammals are fed coffee berries, and after they defecate, their feces are collected, washed, and used to make *kopi luwak* (civet coffee). The action of the civet's stomach enzymes gives the coffee an unrivaled richness of flavor without any of the usual bitterness. As a result, *kopi luwak* is the world's most expensive beverage, costing as much as $1,000 per pound.

Coffee is as big a part of Indo culture as it is in American culture. Street vendors sell everything from coffee candies to instant brews, and people in some outer villages drink it from containers made of coffee leaves—coffee in its own cup.

Indonesian coffee beans are considered the finest in the world, and plants are grown in Sumatra, Java, Bali, Sumbawa, Flores, and even Papua, where fertilizer and pesticides are unknown. If you like coffee, Indo is king. But I let rich coffee freaks buy that wild toddy-cat roast....

Here are some of the ways Indonesians drink their coffee:

Kopi Jahe: Coffee mixed with ginger and palm sugar, promoted as an herbal medication for alleviating flu.

Kopi Bumbu: Brewed coffee with sugar, cinnamon, cardamom, and cloves. This blend was introduced to Sumatra by Middle Eastern traders in the seventeenth century.

Kopi Sereh: Coffee with lemongrass, an aromatic seasoning that Indonesians purport gives freshness to the body.

Kopi Lethok: Flavored with coconut milk and palm sugar, this east Java recipe is sometimes called coffee toddy, not for its alcohol but for the toddy cats—but, of course, you can add a shot of whiskey if you wish.

Gado Gado
Blanched Vegetables in Peanut Sauce

If this Sumatran salad potpourri sounds odd to your Western palate, don't be put off. You won't find a tastier way to eat your vegetables.

SERVES 6

PEANUT SAUCE

1 tablespoon peanut oil
1 small sweet Maui onion, slivered
2 cloves garlic, slivered
1 large chile pepper, minced
1½ teaspoons Indonesian shrimp paste
2 tablespoons soy sauce

1 tablespoon lemon juice
12 ounces crunchy peanut butter
¼ cup palm or dark brown sugar
¾ cup unsweetened coconut milk
½ cup water

VEGETABLES

6 tablespoons peanut oil, for frying
1 pound medium Yukon gold potatoes, peeled
   and cut into ¼-inch slices
1 pound green beans, trimmed and cut into
   2-inch pieces
2 carrots, cut into ¼-inch slices (about 1 cup)
¼ head green cabbage, cored and cut into
   2-inch pieces

2 cups bean sprouts
3 cups spinach, trimmed and washed
Small bunch watercress, trimmed and
   washed, chilled until ready for plating
1 green cucumber, sliced diagonally
   ⅛ inch thick
15 Indonesian shrimp chips, fried
3 hard-boiled eggs, peeled and halved

First, make the peanut sauce. Heat oil in a 12-inch nonstick wok or skillet over medium heat, and stir-fry onion until soft, about 3 minutes. Add garlic and chile, and gently fry for about 1 minute; remove and set aside.

Add shrimp paste to wok and fry, crushing it with the back of a spoon. Pour in soy sauce and lemon juice and mix to combine. Remove from heat and spoon in peanut butter. Stir until well blended. Let cool and transfer mixture to food processor. Add sugar and garlic-chile mixture and purée into a paste.

Transfer paste back to wok and add coconut milk. Simmer over medium-low heat, stirring constantly, until mixture begins to separate, about 5 to 7 minutes. Stir in water and simmer until sauce is thickened, 2 to 3 minutes. Remove from heat and set aside while you cook vegetables.

Prepare the vegetables: Heat 6 tablespoons peanut oil in a 6-quart saucepan until very hot; when oil begins to pop, spoon in potatoes. Fry potatoes until golden, 3 to 4 minutes. Using a slotted spoon, transfer to colander to drain.

Bring a large pot of water to a boil and add green beans and carrots. Blanch for 2 minutes, then add cabbage and cook for another minute. Add bean sprouts and spinach, and blanch for a second or two. Drain vegetables in a colander.

Arrange a layer of chilled watercress in a large salad bowl. Add potatoes and vegetables. Top with cucumber, fried shrimp chips, and eggs. Pour sauce over all and serve.

PERU
An Emerging Power in Surfing & Culinary Culture

The sport of surfing may have been created in Hawaii and spawned in California, but nowhere will you find more passionate wave riders than in Peru. The country's 1,400-mile coastline is a vast, diverse wave field, with big-wave breaks, endless left points, powerful beach breaks, and well-groomed rock reefs.

My early travels to Chicama, home to the world's longest left point, was only matched by the sight of the Andes Mountains framing ancient Machu Picchu. Seeing this culture's magnificent pre-Columbian ruins was fascinating. But witnessing the Peruvian surfers in their little reed fishing boats—riding waves as their forefathers did two millennia ago—was a revelation.

As for food, the Peruvian palate, influenced by Chinese techniques and flavors, is quite sophisticated, and Peru's chefs are now some of the most respected in the world. Peru has more than 4,000 potato varieties alone, and natives as well as visitors have become obsessed with tasting the multitude of variations here. And around the globe, Peruvian restaurants are sprouting up like Cuzco's ancient Inca mushrooms. Yes, Peruvians love to eat and drink—almost as much as they love to surf.

Chicama waves

Peruvian Hot Sauce 220

Peruvian Pisco Sour 223

Causa 224
Crab, Avocado & Mashed Potato Terrine

Ceviche de Salmón y Langostinas Peruano 229
Citrus Shrimp & Salmon Ceviche

Alto Pico Salad 231

Peruvian Quinoa Honey Shrimp 233

Quinoa Trail Mix Bars 235

Chaufa 236
Peruvian-Style Chinese Fried Rice

Ají de Gallina 239
Creamed Spicy Chicken

Fresh clams served straight from the brine

HUANCHACO, TRUJILLO
Riding the Little Reed Horses

When the reed canoes called *caballitos de totora* ("little reed horses") move through the swells, they are continuing a tradition that Peruvian fishermen have employed for more than 3,000 years. These high-prow reed watercraft are named for the way they appear to ride like horses over the crest of each wave—perhaps the very first to do so in surfing history. And they ride the waves back in as well, light sparkling from the wet reeds, rippling like muscles as they surge forward.

These canoes are everywhere in the surf-centric town of Huanchaco, a last outpost on the surf frontier. Even though it's got a party atmosphere, the 800 yards of peaks and reefs—clean and consistent—are almost never crowded. In 2012, the surf preservation organization Save the Waves declared this spot a World Surfing Reserve, an honor that should make it as highly regarded for its surf as it is for its ceviche.

Not far from that little surf town is Chan Chan, the excavated remains of South America's largest pre-Columbian city. For centuries, the Chimu people were an ocean-oriented civilization built around fishing and diving. With no harbor, Chimu seafarers rode their boats through the surf, took their catch, and returned to beach onto the sand not fifty yards from the ocean-facing entrance of the city. Their reed boats were the same ones we saw being ridden in Huanchaco today. Were the Chimu the world's first wave riders? That question will be debated for years to come.

Peruvian Hot Sauce

They may look like small, sweet red bell peppers, but rocoto peppers are in fact quite spicy. The paste made from these South American chiles is available online.

MAKES ABOUT ¾ CUP

2 to 4 tablespoons rocoto chile paste
½ cup light mayonnaise
Juice of 1 lime
1 tablespoon vinegar

2 tablespoons lemon juice
1 teaspoon sugar
½ teaspoon powdered mustard
Sea salt and freshly ground pepper, to taste

Whisk together 2 tablespoons chile paste, mayonnaise, lime, vinegar, lemon juice, sugar, and powdered mustard in a small bowl. Taste and add more chile paste if your palate can handle it, and add salt and pepper if you think it's needed. Store in refrigerator until ready to use.

Kane Ramos surfing a caballitos de totora

CLUB WAIKIKI, MIRAFLORES

Club Waikiki

Peru is one of the top ten surf nations in the world, and Club Waikiki is the country's international surf embassy. Founded in 1942 when Carlos Dogny was introduced to Duke Kahanamoku in Hawaii, this opulent beach club overlooks the gentle, rolling waves of the surf world's most exclusive enclave. With a $15,000 membership fee, Club Waikiki is obviously not your average surf club. Over the years the stories coming from the world's top surfers about their exploits at Club Waikiki could fill a book—and not one about cooking.

Located in Miraflores, the ritziest section of Lima, the club has counted most of Peru's great surfers as members. Its exclusivity is probably matched only by Honolulu's Outrigger Canoe Club. But it's not snooty—if you get an invitation to visit, you'll discover that there are no more gracious hosts, nor more hospitable people, than Peruvian surfers.

The pisco sour, the national cocktail, is served at Club Waikiki's poolside bar. You won't find a better one in Lima.

Peru has an endless coastline of waves.

Peruvian Pisco Sour

Pisco is a high-proof spirit made from fermented grape juice distilled into an amber-colored brandy of considerable kick. The other ingredients in a pisco sour make it almost painless to drink. Peruvians often tell me that one pisco sour is perfect, two is too many, and four will make you speak fluent Spanish even if you've never heard the language.

Note: To make a simple syrup, combine equal amounts of water and sugar in a saucepan, bring to a boil, and when the sugar is completely dissolved, cool and use.

MAKES 1 COCKTAIL

2 ounces key lime juice
1 tablespoon egg white
3 ounces Peruvian pisco

1½ ounces simple syrup
¼ cup crushed ice
2 to 3 drops Angostura bitters

In a blender, combine key lime juice with egg white. Add pisco, simple syrup, and ice, and blend at high speed until frothy. Pour into a sour cocktail glass, top with a few drops of bitters, and serve.

CLUB WAIKIKI, MIRAFLORES

Spreading Aloha from Waikiki to Club Waikiki

Legendary surfer George Downing had a huge influence on the development of Peruvian surf culture. A Renaissance waterman, George was instrumental in designing surfboards, pioneering big-wave riding, creating competition rules and judging systems, exploring new surf spots, and expanding surf travel back when it was nascent.

First traveling to Peru in 1955, George won the country's championship and established lifelong relationships with wealthy, ocean-loving Peruvians. He returned to Peru in 1961 and '65, winning the Peruvian championship both times. Both his contest acumen and his prowess in big waves changed the way the Latin surfers approached wave riding. Sent as Hawaii's surfing ambassador at the invitation of Peru's surfing elite—aka, the members of Club Waikiki—he returned many times to coach, develop competitive surfboards, and share aloha with South Americans. George began a long friendship between the Hawaiian and Peruvian surf cultures that remains to this day.

Causa
Crab, Avocado & Mashed Potato Terrine

There are some 4,000 varieties of potato in Peru. *Causa* is the Spanish derivation for an old Incan Quechua word, *kausaq*, which means "giver of life," another name for the potato. During the struggle for Peru's independence, this became the national dish—and nicknamed for their great cause—or *la causa*.

Packed (literally) with power nutrients, this dish is a complete meal in itself, and it's no more difficult or time-consuming to make than a triple-decker sandwich. This version—with crab and avocado—is especially delicious.

Note: Ají amarillo is a spicy yellow pepper grown all over Peru. The paste is available online.

SERVES 6

2½ pounds Yukon gold potatoes, peeled,
  cooked, and mashed
⅓ cup canola oil
¼ cup fresh lime or lemon juice
3 tablespoons ají amarillo chile paste
  (or other yellow chile paste)
Sea salt and freshly ground pepper, to taste

½ cup plain nonfat Greek yogurt
Juice of 3 to 4 key limes
12 ounces fresh crabmeat, shredded
1 large ripe avocado
1 tablespoon vegetable oil

TOPPING

6 teaspoons light sour cream
2 hard-boiled eggs, sliced into rounds
6 black Kalamata olives, pitted

½ red bell pepper, diced
1 small ripe avocado
6 sprigs of rosemary, for garnish

Place potatoes in a mixing bowl as soon as they are cooked and mashed. Stir in oil, citrus juice, and ají amarillo chile paste, adding salt and pepper to taste. Combine well so color is uniform. The mashed potatoes should now be a colorful yellow. Refrigerate mixture until cold and stiff.

In a separate mixing bowl, combine yogurt with lime juice and shredded crabmeat and mix well. Add salt and pepper to taste and refrigerate until cold and stiff.

Peel, pit, and cut avocado into ½-inch slices. Cover with plastic wrap and chill well.

Lightly oil a short, wide cocktail glass (about 3 inches tall and 3 inches wide at top). Line glass with plastic wrap, pressing it down to fit the dish. Repeat with 5 other glasses. Now you are ready to start layering the ingredients.

First add a layer of very cold, very stiff potatoes (about 1/2 inch, or one-sixth of depth of glass). Next, add a few avocado slices, making sure to cover outside edges of potato layer. Add a second layer of potato, pressing down gently to compact. Now add a layer of crab mixture and press down firmly. Add more avocado slices. Finally, add a third layer of potato mixture; you should reach the top of the glass. Press down firmly so all layers are tight.

Lay a small salad plate upside down over top of causa glass. Using both hands, flip both glass and plate over, letting causa fall onto plate. Remove and discard plastic wrap. Repeat for remainder of causas. When all causas are plated, mound a teaspoon of sour cream on each. Top with hard-boiled eggs, olives, and diced red peppers. Peel, pit, and dice avocado and use it as final garnish to causas.

Spear a sprig of rosemary into each causa to add a little Incan drama to the dish.

CABO BLANCO, PIURA

A Great Wave, a Cautionary Tale & a (Hopefully) Good Ending

Cabo Blanco, where we were headed not long ago, had a reputation that preceded it. Surf journalist Steve Barilotti had told me a few years earlier that this bedraggled little fishing village was famous for two things: 1) Hemingway had once fished for marlin here; and 2) it was home to Panic Point, a screaming left-breaking barrel of a wave that stands up and peels directly in front of the town's anchorage. Steve also warned me back then that Hemingway and Cabo Blanco had three other features in common: Both were legends, both had their pictures tacked to the walls of the Black Marlin—and both were quite dead.

He didn't say why this once-world-renowned seaside resort famous for big-game fish—where Marilyn Monroe, John Wayne, and Paul Newman had frolicked in the shorebreak—became a ghost town that almost lost everything. But when I visited, I learned the answer, and it's a cautionary tale for all ocean lovers.

The fish once came to this particular spot, where the cold waters of the Humboldt Current collide with the warm waters from the Pacific Equatorial Countercurrent, because of the surges of plankton that rushed to the surface. The anchovies would prey on the plankton; they, in turn, were food for marlin, squid, and swordfish. But then the hundreds of millions of anchovies and other small fish disappeared, overfished in what had become a desert of the sea. The big fish moved on, and Cabo Blanco faded to the brink of oblivion.

If not for its surf break, which attracted a life-support visitor base, the whole coastline would have become Peru's rust belt. It was barely hanging on. But now it looks like help is coming. In 2015, Peruvian President Ollanta Humala—as part of a plan to protect the country's vast shoreline and deep rain forests—declared this stretch a conservation area. Included are plans to create a marine reserve in Cabo Blanco. The first marine reserve in the tropical Pacific, it would protect the 238 species of fish, sixty-eight species of crustacean, and nineteen species of whales that live there. Such endangered species as leatherback turtles and blue whales would be more effectively preserved in the proposed 4,000-square-mile reserve and allow the overfished fish stocks to recover.

Onshore, Hemingway's beloved Cabo Blanco Fishing Club is to be restored by an environmental hotel company. His forty-two-foot boat, *Miss Texas*, has already been rebuilt, and there are plans to reintroduce sustainable catch-and-release sport fishing for big-game hunters.

And the Black Marlin Restaurant, where all the stars ate and drank, has been restored and is now operational—and serves some pretty tasty seafood.

Cabo Blanco, the once and future world paradise of fishing

Ceviche de Salmón y Langostinas Peruano
Citrus Shrimp & Salmon Ceviche

In most coastal villages and towns, you can find this dish being served in small stands along the beach, sometimes so fresh, they don't even add the marinade. The key to great ceviche is excellent-grade, perfectly fresh seafood. Done right, it's as good as the best sushi! If you like less heat, use less hot pepper. If you like more heat, double the peppers—and prepare for hiccups.

SERVES 6

3 salmon fillets (about 1 pound), deboned and skin removed
12 large shrimp (about ½ pound), peeled and deveined
½ cup chopped orange
1 cup fresh lime juice, divided
2 cloves garlic, finely chopped
1 jalapeño, seeded and diced
Sea salt and freshly ground pepper, to taste
½ small red onion, slivered

1 cup fresh lemon juice
¼ cup chopped fresh cilantro
1 hot pepper (ideally red or green), seeded and sliced into long, thin slivers
1 ounce Peruvian pisco
6 Kalamata olives, pitted
6 small sweet red peppers, seeded and chopped
1 cooked ear of corn on the cob, cut into 6 (½-inch-thick) rounds

Slice salmon into ½-inch-wide x 2-inch-long strips. Chop shrimp into ½-inch chunks.

Combine orange pulp, ½ cup lime juice, garlic, jalapeño, salt, and pepper in a blender and purée. In a baking dish, coat salmon with this mixture, then add in shrimp and the remaining ½ cup lime juice. Cover with plastic wrap, refrigerate, and marinate until fish is opaque, at least 4 hours.

Marinate red onion slices in lemon juice for about an hour.

Remove seafood from refrigerator and drain marinade. Add cilantro, hot pepper, and marinated onion, and mix. Refrigerate until ready to serve.

To serve, place ceviche on a platter, drizzle pisco over seafood, and surround with olives, red peppers, and corn rounds.

PICO ALTO, PUNTA HERMOSA
Big Peak, Beautiful Point

Punta Hermosa ("beautiful point"), the charming but slightly disheveled beach village twenty miles outside the capital of Lima, has two natural wonders: the big-wave spot at Pico Alto and Peruvian world champion Sofia Mulanovich.

The site of many major contests, Punta Hermosa has a dozen breaks that range from mellow, sheltered beginners' waves to forty-foot-plus mountains. It's most famous for Pico Alto, the big peak, just around the corner from the other breaks. Big-wave master Gary Linden rode a four-story monster here and knows its power. "I don't know another like it for speed and length," he told me. Peruvian legend and 1965 World Champion Felipe Pomar agrees. And he ought to know. Felipe and Pitty Block were getting ready to paddle out when a *terremoto* (powerful earthquake) hit. After it was over and they collected themselves, they paddled out with high hopes of catching a big tsunami wave. They got more than they bargained for, and were thankful to make it back to shore with their lives.

As for Sofia, when she won the women's world championship at the Billabong Pro at Honolua Bay, Maui, I was the media director responsible for getting the news out to the world. While I was sending out press releases, the incoming live-streaming videos from Peru showed hundreds of thousands of people cheering in the country's sports bars. Before we had completed the trophy ceremonies, I'd received a telegram of congratulations for her—from the president of Peru. In her country, Sophia is a celebrity on the scale of Beyoncé in America.

Alto Pico Salad

This colorful, healthy salad is elegant but simple, and it's built around foods that are grown in Peru. Tomatoes are native to the Andes region, and nearly ninety percent of the artichoke hearts consumed in the US are grown in Peru, mostly near the coast. Peruvian asparagus is a booming farm product, a result of farmers replacing coca plants with this delicious vegetable. Pink peppercorns come from the Peruvian pepper tree, another native of the Andes. Peruvian pink mountain salt, which you can find in a gourmet store or online, is harvested by hand from an ancient natural spring located at 10,000 feet in the Andes. The warm spring water seeps into terraced salt ponds and crystallizes the salt. The taste is worth the effort to find it.

SERVES 6

4 tomatoes, sliced

18 asparagus spears, grilled

3 ripe but firm avocados, peeled, pitted, and sliced

2 jars roasted artichoke hearts (about 12), drained and halved, liquid reserved

1 head butter lettuce, torn into small (2-inch) pieces

2 tablespoons white wine vinegar

1 teaspoon coarse sea salt (preferably Peruvian pink mountain)

1 teaspoon freshly cracked peppercorns (preferably Peruvian)

Set out a large oval platter. Place tomato slices around the platter, alternating asparagus spears between tomatoes with tips facing outward. Place avocado slices and artichoke hearts on tomatoes. Mound butter lettuce in center of platter.

Drizzle with about 1/4 cup of the reserved artichoke oil and porur vinegar over mixture. Sprinkle with salt and a heavy dose of freshly cracked pepper, and serve.

A Peruvian-Chinese-Italian Surfer Joint

You know you're in good hands in the kitchen when a Peruvian restaurant named Trattoria Don Angelo has amazing Chinese food. It's one of those great surf haunts found in beach towns worldwide, where you're likely to see many of the other surfers in town eating. When I visited Pico Alto with Snips Parsons, whose record-setting seventy-two-foot wave won him the XXL biggest wave award, and Chris "Heff" Heffner, the funniest guy at Billabong, we'd order the restaurant's famed Alto Pico Salad for the whole table to share.

MIRAFLORES, LIMA
Coca, Cocoa, Quinoa, Cuzco & Conquistadors

During one memorable trip to Peru, we went to Miraflores, an upscale coastal suburb of Lima, the night before we were to depart for a hike into Machu Picchu via the Inca trail. A long row of restaurants hung over the high cliffs, each offering nouvelle Peruvian cuisine, dramatic views of the Pacific, and the best pisco sours in the city. There's something about the combination of egg whites, lime juice, and brandy that makes the stuff go down so easily. It's like eating ice cream. My mistake was ordering four scoops.

Taking down most of the chairs and several tables while exiting the restaurant should have been a forewarning that sprinting up three flights of stairs was probably not a great idea. My foot missed a step, hitting the front edge, and my heel whipped directly under a stair, extending my entire weight onto the Achilles tendon. I felt a sharp yank on my fibula—and the ugly sound of a long strand of sinew snapping flat and hard, like a mousetrap.

I spent the next two days getting physician-administered shots in my torn Achilles while sipping hot chocolate laced with coca leaf tea. When brought back to Europe to make chocolate, cocoa revolutionized the gastronomic world. In no other way has nature concentrated such a wealth of delicious nourishment into such a small thing as the cocoa bean.

As for coca leaf tea, it's a tasty, legal painkiller and energy booster that's served everywhere in Peru. The Incas used the coca leaf for thousands of years as an antidote for altitude sickness and hunger.

I sated my own appetite with prawns dipped in honey and quinoa. The Incas thought of quinoa the way Mexicans think of tortillas and Moroccans think of couscous—it pretty much goes with everything. Healthier than most other grains, quinoa is low in cholesterol, loaded with nutrients, and a complete protein. Unfortunately, as evidence of a cultural blind spot the size of the Amazon, Conquistadors destroyed most of Peru's native quinoa crops and replaced them with rice. Thankfully, now it's making a comeback.

Whatever. Ignoring the advice of the physician and the unrelenting pain in my upper heel, I threw my bag in the car with my friends and headed for Cusco, gateway through the sacred valley. The capital of the Inca Empire until the sixteenth-century Spanish conquest, it's an architectural gemstone. I wasn't going to miss Machu Picchu.

Peruvian Quinoa Honey Shrimp

Modern Peruvian food is one of the great fusion cuisines to come out of the last decade. Already immersed in Chinese cooking, Peruvians have now married Asian, Incan, European, and American influences into a first-rate culinary tradition all its own.

SERVES 6

1 cup all-purpose flour
⅔ cup water
1 large egg, lightly beaten
16 colossal shrimp (about 1 pound), shelled
   and deveined
6 tablespoons cornstarch
Grapeseed oil

1 tablespoon light sesame oil
¼ cup honey
½ cup cooked quinoa
Sesame seeds, to taste
3 green onions, green ends only, cut into
   ¼-inch dice

Sift flour into a bowl. Add water and egg, and beat gently to a smooth batter. Set aside for ten minutes.

Meanwhile, coat shrimp in cornstarch. Shake off any excess. Add shrimp to batter and coat well.

Heat grapeseed oil in wok over high heat until almost smoking. Add shrimp, a few at a time, until batter is golden, about 3 to 4 minutes. Remove shrimp, drain on paper towels, and keep warm. Continue until all shrimp are fried. Carefully remove hot oil from wok and discard.

Gently heat sesame oil in wok. Add honey and quinoa, and stir together. Combine shrimp with quinoa mixture and toss well. Sprinkle sesame seeds and green onions over shrimp. Serve hot.

MACHU PICCHU, CUSCO
Inca Deal

What drove the Incas to build the City in the Clouds, rediscovered only a century ago? Along with the sacred religious traditions full of vestal virgins and astronomical observatories, it also had a practical purpose: access to exotic food products. Machu Picchu's combination of altitude and closeness to the Amazon rain forest gave the Incas a source for cocoa leaves, fruits, vegetables, and healing herbs. In these high altitudes, potatoes, quinoa, and guinea pigs proliferate, and the coastal zone supplied fish and seafood; the famous Inca Chasqui runners brought Pacific fish all the way to Cusco, 11,000 feet up the Andes.

As you thread the long, bony spine of the Andes along the Inca Trail, nothing can prepare you for the sheer scale of Machu Picchu's majesty. Condors soar over distant mountains. Nine thousand feet up, it's still warmer than most California winter nights. The Amazon basin keeps the area temperate, even though on the Argentinean side of this jagged range, there are glaciers. From the fifteenth-century capital of Cusco, a train snakes along the riverbed of what the Incas called the sacred valley—a curving route that looked to them like the mirror image of the Milky Way's swath of stars. That path also connected the Amazon, the desert coast, and the Andes so that the bounty of exotic food could be distributed throughout the empire. So while Machu Picchu's Temple of the Sun may have been the heart of their world, the intricate irrigated terraces indicate that they also understood that an empire travels on its belly.

Machu Picchu: must be the clouds in my eyes

Quinoa Trail Mix Bars

These super-tasty health bars are easy to make, even for the non-baker, and provide a combo of superfoods that will fuel strenuous activity. We ate them on the hike through Machu Picchu, where the 9,000-foot elevation requires more energy and oxygenation.

MAKES 24 BARS

1¾ cups water

1 cup quinoa

1 cup packed brown sugar

1 cup cornstarch

1 teaspoon baking powder

½ teaspoon baking soda

1 teaspoon ground cinnamon

¼ teaspoon grated nutmeg

½ cup dried cranberries

½ cup chopped apricots

½ cup chopped walnuts

½ cup fresh orange juice

½ cup (1 stick) unsalted butter, melted

2 teaspoons vanilla extract

3 eggs, lightly beaten

Heat water to boiling, pour in quinoa, and cook for about 12 minutes. Remove from heat and let cool.

Butter and flour a 9 x 13-inch baking pan. Combine brown sugar, cornstarch, baking powder, baking soda, cinnamon, nutmeg, cranberries, apricots, and walnuts in a large bowl, and mix well. Pour in cooked quinoa, then add orange juice, butter, vanilla, and eggs. Stir all ingredients vigorously until mixture is smooth.

Scrape into prepared baking pan and spread evenly. Bake on top rack of oven until a fork piercing the center comes out clean, about 45 minutes.

After pan has cooled, cut into 24 bars. Enjoy as a dessert or as an energy booster on long hikes or surf sessions—and as a healthy, safe substitute for Peruvian marching powder.

Chaufa
Peruvian-Style Chinese Fried Rice

Adding or substituting ingredients to any stir-fried rice is simple and delicious. Typical additions include shredded cabbage, sliced yellow squash, and finely diced celery. Use whatever you'd like to make this dish your own.

SERVES 6

3 cups basmati rice
Chinese soy sauce, as needed
2 teaspoons chopped fresh garlic, divided
2 teaspoons chopped fresh ginger, divided
½ teaspoon black bean sauce
1 teaspoon Chinese five-spice powder
1 jalapeño or other chile, chopped

1 chicken breast, cut into ¼-inch strips
4 large eggs
Sea salt and freshly ground pepper, to taste
Canola oil
½ cup peas and diced carrots
½ cup chopped green onions

Cook rice according to package instructions, adding 1 tablespoon soy sauce to the water.

While rice is cooking, stir together 1 teaspoon garlic, 1 teaspoon ginger, black bean sauce, five-spice powder, chile, and 1 tablespoon (or to taste) soy sauce in a medium bowl. Add chicken strips, toss to combine, and set aside.

Beat eggs with salt and pepper to taste and scramble in a frying pan, cooking until set but still soft. Set aside.

Heat a tablespoon or so of oil in a wok or large skillet over high heat. Add chicken and cook, stirring. Add remaining garlic, ginger, peas, and carrots, and cook, stirring, until chicken is cooked. Stir in cooked rice and mix well, tasting and adding salt and pepper, or more soy sauce if needed. Remove from heat, add chopped green onions, and serve.

EL CENTRO, LIMA

Peking in Peru?

A surprising delight on my first visit to Peru were the *chifa* restaurants found everywhere on the bustling streets of Lima. Peruvian Chinese food may seem odd to *norteamericanos,* but it's actually an authentic part of Andean cooking history.

As slavery became outlawed in the mid- to late-nineteenth century, a severe labor shortage hit the Peruvian sugar plantations and mines. In the decades that followed, tens of thousands of Chinese workers immigrated to Peru, bringing their spices, recipes, and cooking techniques.

Chinese immigrants introduced their cuisine to the local population with great success. In Peru they opened chifas, serving typical Chinese dishes but substituting many South American ingredients, like pineapple and ají amarillo. They became hugely popular, assimilating into Peruvian cuisine the way Mexican food has become an integral part of California's culinary tradition.

Ají de Gallina
Creamed Spicy Chicken

Ají de Gallina is Peruvian cooking at its best. Mildly spicy from its bright yellow ají amarillo peppers and rich from the walnut cream sauce, it's one of the classics of Peruvian cuisine. It's filling and satisfying and will be a hit with anybody familiar with Peru—or not.

Note: Frozen yellow ají peppers and ají amarillo paste are available at Latin food markets or online. You can substitute another hot chile pepper for ají amarillo peppers, and add a spoonful of turmeric for color.

SERVES 6

4 yellow potatoes	2 large red bell peppers, cut into 2-inch pieces
4 slices white bread	1 large onion, diced
¾ cup evaporated milk	2 cloves garlic, minced
3 large chicken breasts	3 tablespoons chopped walnuts
4 cups chicken stock	3 tablespoons grated parmesan cheese
3 yellow ají amarillo peppers	2 hard-boiled eggs, sliced
½ cup vegetable oil	12 Kalamata olives, pitted

Salt 2 quarts water and cook potatoes in water until tender when pierced with a fork. Drain, let potatoes cool, then peel and cut into quarters. Cover potatoes and place in a bowl in refrigerator to prevent browning.

In a small bowl, soak bread in evaporated milk. Set aside.

In a large stockpot, cook chicken breasts in chicken stock, simmering for 10 to 15 minutes, until chicken is just barely cooked through. Set chicken aside in a bowl. Reserve 2 cups of the broth.

Remove stems and seeds from ají peppers. In a blender, process peppers with vegetable oil until smooth.

In a large pan over medium-high heat, sauté red bell peppers and onion with the puréed pepper mixture, until onions are soft and golden. Add garlic and sauté for another minute, or until garlic is fragrant. Remove from heat and set aside. Pull out 12 pieces of red bell pepper to reserve for garnish.

Shred the cooled chicken into bite-size pieces and set aside.

In a blender, purée evaporated milk-and-bread mixture, then slowly add nuts, cooked onion/bell pepper mixture, and parmesan cheese, processing until smooth. Return blended mixture to pan, and add 1 1/2 cups reserved chicken stock. Simmer on low until hot, then stir in shredded chicken. Heat until warmed through, adding more chicken stock if sauce is too thick.

Bring potatoes back to room temperature, and serve chicken on a bed of rice, garnished with potatoes, reserved bell peppers, slices of hard-boiled egg, and olives.

CHICAMA, NORTHERN COAST
Chicama Time

Once the province of a sophisticated ancient sea culture, and then a sugar-refining locale, the remote fishing village of Chicama now carries a foreboding vagueness, a region whose purpose outside of a surfer's obvious attraction is hard to discern. But for the surfer, it's easy to discern—there's a perfectly peeling wave that breaks in football-field sections.

Sitting on the bluff above the long scimitar curve of desert coast, my friends and I are watching the waves break, and I'm getting ready to time the length of one from beginning to end. How long do these waves keep going? The entire field of lineup—stretching from the outer point to the promontory just past a resort—is slightly over a mile and a quarter. I check my watch to time the biggest wave that's about to break over the outer point.

Chicama's wave is considered to be the longest on the planet. It's a real-life version of the fantasy doodles sketched countless times in every adolescent surfer's math notebook (while appearing to follow the algebraic procedure being chalked on the blackboard). This coastal bluff protruding onto the southeastern Pacific Ocean has created a rare topography that allows a wave to sometimes break uninterrupted from the southerly outside point to the dilapidated pier below the northern edge of the village.

It looks like a hundred sketches, actually, moving across a stationary ocean backdrop, an endless step-and-repeat design that progresses from one still image to the next. The falling lip of the peeling wave moves rapid-fire, rather like early motion-picture animation. In the mauve-blue-gray light, it does not look real.

Although four intrepid Peruvians are credited with discovering Chicama's long walls in 1965, it is likely that other wave riders surfed there much earlier. A few years ago, a Peruvian surfer visited Casa Grande, Peru's largest sugar plantation, located in the Chicama River Valley not far from the coast. There he found a number of wooden surfboards in the plantation's old warehouses. Made from Peruvian balsa, they appear to be from the 1930s or earlier. No doubt sugar plantation staff members from Hawaii visited or worked at Casa Grande during that period. To enjoy the perfect point break, they built surfboards and, most probably, rode them in solitary splendor. If they were riding the waves, they kept them secret for some three decades. Even now, Chicama's storied lineup remains uncrowded.

As the cracked wind stirs the long, crescent scar of shoreline, I look up, eyes slowly coming into long-distance focus on the lineup. The wave I'm timing continues, unspooling like a white ribbon across a bolt of blue velvet. How long has this damn thing been going now? I glance at my watch, but I can't remember the exact moment I first made a note to time its length. It doesn't exactly matter. In the fast-fading light, this freak of nature is *still breaking*.

Chicama time becomes relative.

Index

Abacos 178
Adour River 50
Africa 44, 56, 108, 128, 172
Agadir 114, 119
Agadir Almond Crunch 119
Agave Lime Dressing 181
Ahern, Jim 110, 123, 124
Aikau, Eddie 6
Ainhoa 57
Ají de Gallina 239
Ala Moana 18
Alas Purwo National Park 200
Aleutian 134
Alfaro, Caliche 98, 247
Alto Pico Salad 231
Anchor Point 110, 112, 128
Anderson, Charlie 69
Andes Mountains 218
Anglet 50, 61
Argan 114
Arroz con Pollo 101
Asparagus 107
Atlantic 30, 36, 40, 108, 121
Australia 16, 64, 73, 208, 210
Avocados Stuffed with Jumbo Shrimp 173
Bahamas 178
Baja Norte 168
Bajan Flying Fish 193
Baked Fish with Almond Sauce 126
Bali 8, 10, 166, 172, 198, 208, 215
Balut 10
Bananas
    Bananas Guadeloupe 197
    Café Haleiwa Banana Pancakes 137
    Tavarua Surf Camp Banana Bread 23
Barbados 176, 187, 189, 192, 193, 196
Barilotti, Steve 226, 247
Basque Country 36-55
Basque Omelet 47
Bay of Biscay 40
Bayonne 40, 47, 50, 57, 60
Beach Break Café 86
Beach, Bruce 66
Beatie, Keiko 181
Beef
    Balinese Beef Satay 206
    Beef-and-Fruit-Stuffed Poblanos with
        Walnut Sauce (Chiles en Nogada) 158
    Chamorro Beef Tinaktak 19
    Machaca & Eggs 167
    Porterhouse Steak with Herb Butter &

    Portuguese Chimichurri 148
Belharra 55
Bent, Buzzy 146
Berber 108, 110
Bethany's Açaí Smoothie 139
Bethany's Papaya Nut Smoothie 139
Biarritz 6, 40, 53
Bidart 62
Billabong 40, 88, 94, 138, 230, 231, 248
Biscay 40, 56, 57
Black Marlin restaurant 226
Blackened Corvina with Garlic Mushroom
    Sauce 90
Blanched Vegetables in Peanut Sauce 216
Block, Pitty 230
Boca Barranca 103
Bonzer 136
Bordeaux 40, 60
Boyum, Bill 200
British Virgin Islands 186
Brown, Gilbert 98
Butternut Squash Soup 112
Cabarete 191
Cabo Blanco 226, 227
Cabo Blanco Fishing Club 226
Cabo San Lucas 164, 166
Caesar Salad 155-157
Caesar's Restaurante 156
Café Haleiwa 136, 137
Café Haleiwa Banana Pancakes 137
Cake
    Gâteau Basque 62
    Palauan Papaya Upside-Down Cake 28
Caicos 182, 183, 189, 190
Caliche's Wishbone Grilled Lobster with
    Coconut Mojo 98
Campbell, Duncan 136, 247
Canal Zone 99
Caribbean 7, 56, 88, 176-196
Caribbean Barry's Barracuda 185
Caribbean Seasoning 192
carnitas 168, 169
Carolines 16
Carroll, Tom 106, 124, 210
Casa Grande 240
Casablanca 82, 126, 129
Castroville 79
Causa 224, 225
Centro 88, 90, 237
Ceviche, Salmon and Shrimp 229
Chadwick, Mark 42
Chamorro 14

Chamorro Beef Tinaktak 19
Chan Chan 220
Chaufa 236
Chefchaouen 128
Cherries & Cheese with Black Cherry Confit 45
Chevrettes à la Vanille et Coco (Tahitian
    Vanilla Shrimp) 27
Chicama 218, 240, 248
Chicken
    Arroz con Pollo 101
    Chaufa (Peruvian fried rice) 236
    Creamed Spicy Chicken (Ají de Gallina)
        239
    Enchiladas Puerto Escondido 161
    Jerk Chicken 180
    Jerk Chicken Salad 180-181
    Pancit Pohnepei (noodles with vegetables
        and chicken) 17
    Poulet Basquaise 52
    Pozole 162
Chiles en Nogada 158
Chimichurri 149
Chimu 220
Chris-Craft 34
Citrus Shrimp & Salmon Ceviche 229
Clarke-Jones, Ross 210
Cloudbreak 22
Club Waikiki 222, 224
Cocktails
    Macuá Cocktail 96-97
    Mai Tai 151
    Mango Margarita 67
    Pamplona Picon Punch 59
    Peruvian Pisco Sour 223
    Ti Punch Rum Cocktail 186
Coconut
    Bethany's Açaí Smoothie 139
    Bethany's Papaya Nut Smoothie 139
    Café Haleiwa Banana Pancakes 137
    Chamorro Beef Tinaktak 19
    Coconut Mojo 98
    Doña Victoria's Kahlúa Coconut Flan 174
    Marrakesh Butternut Squash Soup 112
    Tahitian Vanilla Shrimp 27
coffee (kopi) 215
coleslaw 190
Corinto 104
corvina 89-91, 105
Costa Rica 88, 92, 96, 98, 100, 102, 103,
    138, 172
Costa Rican Coffee-Rubbed Pork with
    Marmalade Glaze 102

Côte Basque Cliffs 50
Cousinat (Vegetable Casserole) 57
Crab
  Crab Bisque 48
  Crab Chipotle Mayonnaise 107
  Crab, Avocado & Mashed Potato Terrine
    (Causa) 224
  Half Moon Bay Salad 79
  Stuffed Yams with Cheese, Crab &
    Tomatoes 31
Creamed Spicy Chicken 239
Croutons, homemade 157
Curaçao 196
Curren, Joe 118
Curren, Teasha 247
Cuzco 218, 232
Daley, Martin 7, 210, 247
Dana Point 18, 72
Dar Bouazza 126
Davis, Leslie & Michael 6, 247
Desserts
  Agadir Almond Crunch 119
  Bananas Guadeloupe 197
  Doña Victoria's Kahlúa Coconut Flan
    174
  Gâteau Basque 62
  Palauan Papaya Upside-Down Cake 28
Divine, Jeff 6, 103, 142, 247
Dogny, Carlos 222
Doheny State Beach 72
Domaine Ilarria of Irouléguy 45
Dominican Republic 191
Doña Victoria's Kahlúa Coconut Flan 174
Dora, Miki 42, 44, 49, 153
Downing, George 224
Eggplant
  Killer Seven-Vegetable Tagine 111
  Roasted Vegetables with Caramelized
    Balsamic Glaze 75
  Spicy-Sweet Shrimp & Eggplant Soup
    210
Eggs
  Basque Omelet 47
  Gado Gado 216
  Machaca & Eggs 167
  Pasta Carbonara 77
El Centro 237
El Salvador 11, 88, 90, 94, 100, 172
Eleuthera 178
Enchiladas Puerto Escondido 161
Essaouira 114, 118, 121
Fallbrook 79
Fare, France 32
Fig Jam Pizza with Goat Cheese, Prosciutto
  & Arugula 69

Fiji 8, 22
Finadene 19
Fish
  Bajan Flying Fish 193
  Baked Fish with Almond Sauce 126
  Black Marlin 226
  Blackened Corvina with Garlic Mushroom
    Sauce 90
  Caribbean Barry's Barracuda 185
  Citrus Shrimp & Salmon Ceviche 229
  Grilled Fish & Vegetable Packet 70
  Macadamia-Crusted Mahi Mahi 133
  Mariscada Salvadorena 94-95
  Ono Poke Bowl 144-145
  Opakapaka Laulau 34
  Pescado Veracruzana 165
  Pink Snapper in Ti Leaves with Spinach
    & Orange-Ginger Sauce 34
  Sashimi Française 33
  Steamed Chile-Ginger Halibut 214
  Tuna Steaks with Onion Marmalade 54
Fitii 32
Five Summer Stories 42
Flan, Coconut 174
Florence, John 76, 77
Flores 11, 94, 215, 248
Foxy's Bar 186
France 6, 8, 36, 40, 44, 50, 52, 53, 60,
  172, 174
French Polynesia 16, 20, 32
Fresno 79
Fruit Salad (Rujak) 209
Gado Gado 216
Gascogne, Pierre 6, 52, 247
Gâteau Basque 62
Gauguin, Paul 26
Guava
  Caribbean Barry's Barracuda 185
  Macuá Cocktail 97
General's Table, The 44
Gibraltar 108
Gilroy 79
Goulimine 122, 123
Grajagan Bay 200
Grambeau, Ted 6
Grande Plage 53
Grigg, Ricky 142
Grilled Asparagus with Crab Chipotle
  Mayonnaise 107
Grilled Fish & Vegetable Packet 70
Guadalajara 174
Guadeloupe Harbor 196
Guam 14, 18, 19, 34, 248
Guedra 112, 113, 124
Guerrero 158, 172

Haleakala Crater 132
Haleiwa 136, 137
Half Moon Bay 78-81
Half Moon Bay Salad 79
Halibut, Steamed Chile-Ginger 214
Hall 7, 26, 132, 134
Hamilton, Bethany 138-139, 140-141, 247
Hamilton, Laird 138
Hamilton, Tom 138
Hana 133
Hanalei Bay 138
Harissa Sauce 125
Hawaii 16, 26, 36, 64, 123, 130-153, 192,
  218, 222, 224, 240
Heffner, Chris 231
Hemingway, Ernest 40, 53, 93, 226
Herb Butter 149
Hinano 30
Ho, Coco 62
Ho'okipa 132
Holmes, Paul 42
Hong Kong 16
Honolua Bay 134, 151, 230
Honolulu 144, 146, 196, 222
Hope, Dale 144
Huahine 14, 20, 32
Huanchaco 220
Humala, Ollanta 226
Hurley Pro 74
Hurley, Bob 76
Hussong's Cantina 170
Iles Purpuraires 121
Inca Trail 232, 234
Indies Trader 7, 88, 90, 99, 104, 106, 108,
  176, 178, 182, 184, 186, 196
Indonesia 16, 154, 164, 198-211
Isla Coiba, Panama 100
Jacó 172
Jalama 164
Japan 16, 130, 212
Java 215
Jeffreys Bay 42, 172
Jemaa el-Fna 112
Jerk Chicken 180-181, 190
Jerk Chicken Salad 180
Kahanamoku, Duke 146, 222
Kahoolawe 132
Kalua Pork with Vegetables 21
Kalua Turkey 143
Kampar River
Kansas 7
Kauai 138
Keaulana, Buffalo 143
Kejawen 200
Kempton, Jim 6, 7, 11, 248

Killer Seven-Vegetable Tagine 111
Kona 134
Kopi (coffees) 215
Korean barbecue 7
Korean Short Ribs 152
Kuau 133
Kuta Beach 198
La Barre 50
Lagundri Bay 202
Lalo 106, 107
Lalo, Joey 106
Lamb
   Merguez Sausage 124
   Moroccan Grilled Lamb Chops with
     Apricots & Prunes 122
Lamno 215
Lanai 132
Las Flores 11, 94
Laverty, Bob 200
Lazy Days Surf Shop 192
Le Sable d'Or 50
Les Alcyons 36
Les Cavaliers 61
Lesser Antilles 196
Lima 222, 230, 232, 237
Linden, Gary 230
Lobster
   Caliche's Wishbone Grilled Lobster with
     Coconut Mojo 98
   Mariscada Salvadorena 94-95
Long, Greg 66, 160, 230, 247
Lopez, Gerry 200
Lovett, Richie 202
Lower Trestles 11, 68, 74
Luau 30
Lunetta, Raphael 8, 247
Maalaea Harbor 132
Macadamia-Crusted Mahi Mahi 133
Macaronis 210
Machaca & Eggs 167
Machado, Rob 98
Machu Picchu 218, 232, 234, 235
Macuá Cocktail 97
Madame Vacher 50
Madame's Moules Marinière 51
Madeira Islands 30
mahi mahi 34, 133
Mai Tai 151
Makaha 142, 153
Makawao 148
Makka Beach 180
Malay 20
Malaysia 16
Malibu 6, 44, 73
Mango

Mango Margarita 67
   Spicy-Sweet Fruit Salad (Rujak) 209
Mango Point 94
Mansfield, Roger 42
Maori 20
Marché Municpal, Tahiti 30
Margarita, Mango 67
Margarita's Village 7, 64-67, 72, 82, 85,
   158, 171, 174, 248
Mariana Trench 14
Mariscada Salvadorena 94-95
Marley, Bob 121, 180, 181
Marrakesh 112, 118, 124
Marrakesh Butternut Squash Soup 112
Marsh, Richard 202
Martinique 186, 196
Maui 21, 35, 73, 75, 132, 134, 138, 148,
   151, 180, 189, 216, 230
Maui Wowie 134
Mauna'olu College 132, 134, 148
Mavericks 10, 58, 78-79
McCabe, Peter 200
McGillivray, Greg 42
McKnight, Bob 166-167
Melanesia 16
Melville, Herman 26
Mentwai Islands 208, 210
Merguez Sausage 124
Merizo Bay 18
Mexico 7, 66, 154-175
Micronesia 16
Miraflores 99, 222, 224, 232
Miss T's Kitchen 180
Mitchell, Jamie 55
Mitchell, Joni 74
Molokai 132, 134
Monroe, Marilyn 226
Moorea 26
Moroccan Blond 128
Moroccan Grilled Lamb Chops with
   Apricots & Prunes 122
Morocco 108-129
Moscoso, Mireya 106
Mount Irvine Bay 184
Mulanovich, Sofia 230
Mundaka 56
Mushrooms & Shrimp 43
Mussels in Garlic Butter 51
Mutiny on the Bounty 26
Nakuru Kuru Malagi 22
Namotu 22
Nassau 178, 196
Navarre 40, 58
Nayarit 174
New Guinea 206

New Zealand 16, 20
Newman, Paul 226
Newport Beach 76, 82, 83
Nias 202-204, 206
Nicaragua 88, 96, 97, 100, 104
Nicoya 92
Niger 123
Noel, Keith 42
Noodles with Vegetables 17
O'Neill 40
Oahu 7, 8, 36, 136, 142, 146, 150
oatmeal 86-87
Oaxaca 85, 154, 158, 160, 161
Oceanside 69, 70, 86, 172
Ocho Rios 180
Ojai 79
Omelet, Basque 47
Ono Poke Bowl 144, 145
Opakapaka Laulau 34
Orange County 68, 158
Pacific Coast Highway 66, 86, 110
Pacific Equatorial Countercurrent 226
Paia 132, 134
Paia Fats 134
pajaro macuá 96, 97
Palauan Papaya Upside-Down Cake 28
Pamplona 40, 53, 58, 59
Pamplona Picon Punch 59
Panama 88, 99, 100, 106, 107
pancakes 137
Pancit Pohnepei 17
Panic Point 226
Papaya
   Bethany's Papaya Nut Smoothie 139
   Caribbean Barry's Barracuda 185
   Palauan Papaya Upside-Down Cake 28
Papeete 30
Papua 215
Parkinson, Joel 179
Parsons, Snips 231
Paskowitz family 87
Pasta & Noodles
   Pancit Pohnepei 17
   Pasta Carbonara 77
Peligroso Tequila 66
Pepes Ikan 214
Peru 218-241
Peruvian Hot Sauce 220
Peruvian Quinoa-Honey Shrimp 233
Peruvian-Style Chinese Fried Rice (Chaufa)
   236
Pescado Veracruzana 165
Pezman, Debbee 6
Pezman, Steve 5-7, 10, 247
pie (Gâteau Basque) 62

Philbin, John 202
Philippines 16, 17, 56, 130, 212
Pico Alto 230, 231
Pine Cay 182
Pineapple
    Bananas Guadeloupe 197
    Bethany's Açai Smoothie 139
    Jerk Chicken Salad 180-181
    Mai Tai 151
    Santo Domingo Sweet Potatoes with
        Pineapple-Rum-Balsamic Glaze 189
    Spicy-Sweet Fruit Salad (Rujak) 209
    Trinidad Coleslaw 190
Pink Snapper in Ti Leaves with Spinach &
    Orange-Ginger Sauce 34
Pintxos 59, 60
Pisco Sour 223
Pisupo 21
Piura 226
Pizza, Fig Jam with Goat Cheese,
    Prosciutto & Arugula 69
Plate Lunch 152
Pleasant Mountain 132
Plengkung 200
Polynesia 16, 20, 32
Poke Bowl 144-145
Pomar, Feiipe 230
Pork
    carnitas 168-169
    Costa Rican Coffee-Rubbed Pork with
        Marmalade Glaze 102
    Kalua Pork with Vegetables (Pisupo) 21
    Pozole 162
    Rice Paper Summer Rolls with Soy-
        Glazed Pork 203
Port de Pêche 126
Porterhouse Steak with Herbed Butter &
    Portuguese Chimichurri 148-149
Portuguese Chimichurri 149
Potato Terrine, Mashed (Causa) 224
Potter's Cay 178, 196
Poulet Basquaise 52
Pozole 162
Privateer 69
Puerto Escondido 154, 160, 161
Pulau Pagai 210
Punalau 134
Punta Bruja 96
Punta Cono 168
Punta Hermosa 230
Punta Mango 94, 95
Punta Maria 169
Punta Mita 174
Punta Negra 169
Punta Perfecta 166

Punta Rocosa 169
Punta Rosarito 168, 169
Punta Santa Rosalillita 169
Pyrenees 40, 45, 57
Quesadilla Kempton 85
Quiksilver 6, 7, 40, 88, 166, 176, 188,
    210, 247, 248
Quinoa Trail Mix Bars 235
Rarick, Randy 142
Raymond, Bruce 210
Red City 124
Redondo Beach 72
Reefcheck Program 176
Rell Sunn's Kalua Turkey 143
Rice
    Arroz con Pollo 101
    Peruvian-Style Chinese Fried Rice
        (Chaufa) 236
    Plate Lunch 152
    Salad Taghazout 115
Rice Paper Summer Rolls with Soy-Glazed
    Pork 203
Rif Mountains 128
Rip Curl 40
Roasted Vegetables with Caramelized
    Balsamic Glaze 75
Rosemary Sea Scallops with Tamarind-
    Olive Sauce 183
Rotherham, Bob 90, 172
Rujak 209
Sáenz, Edmundo 97
Safi 124, 126
Sahara 108, 123, 126
Saint-Jean-de-Luz 54, 55
Salad Bar 146-147
Salad Taghazout 115
Salade Aquitaine 41
Salads
    Alto Pico Salad 231
    Blanched Vegetables in Peanut Sauce
        (Gado Gado) 216
    Caesar Salad 155-157
    Half Moon Bay Salad 79
    Salad Bar 146-147
    Salad Taghazout 115
    Salade Aquitaine 41
    Spicy-Sweet Fruit Salad (Rujak) 209
salmon 229
salsa 105
Salvadoran Seafood Soup (Mariscada) 95
San Clemente 6, 7, 64, 66, 68, 72, 82,
    86, 248
San Clemente Café 86
San Diego 6, 56, 168, 172
San Fermín 58

San Francisco 56
San José del Cabo 164
San Onofre 10, 74, 87, 248
San Sebastián 44, 60
Santa Barbara 79
Santo Domingo 189, 196
Santo Domingo Sweet Potatoes with
    Pineapple-Rum-Balsamic Glaze 189
Sashimi Française 33
satay 206
Sauces & Dressings
    Agave Lime Dressing 181
    Almond Sauce 126
    Aquitaine Dressing 41
    Finadene 19
    Gado Gado (Peanut Sauce) 216
    Garlic Mushroom Sauce 90
    Harissa Sauce 125
    Herb Butter 149
    Onion Marmalade 54
    Orange-Ginger Sauce 34
    Peruvian Hot Sauce 220
    Portuguese Chimichurri 149
    Surfer's Choice teriyaki sauce 70
    Sweet Chile Sauce 214
    Tamarind-Olive Sauce 183
    Tomato Chermoula Sauce 117
    Trinidad Dressing 190
Sausage, Merguez 124
Scallops with Tamarind-Olive Sauce 183
Schlea, Brent 134, 247
Seafood
    Avocados Stuffed with Jumbo Shrimp
        173
    Caliche's Wishbone Grilled Lobster with
        Coconut Mojo 98
    Citrus Shrimp & Salmon Ceviche 229
    Crab, Avocado & Mashed Potato Terrine
        (Causa) 224
    Crab Bisque 44, 48
    Crab Chipotle Mayonnaise 107
    Half Moon Bay Salad 79
    Mushrooms & Shrimp (Zurrukatuna) 43
    Mussels in Garlic Butter (Moules
    Marinière) 51
    Peruvian Quinoa-Honey Shrimp 233
    Rosemary Sea Scallops with Tamarind-
        Olive Sauce 183
    Salvadoran Seafood Soup 95
    Shrimp Phyllo Purses with Tomato
    Chermoula Sauce 116
    Spicy-Sweet Shrimp & Eggplant Soup
        (Terung Lodeh) 210
    Stuffed Yams with Cheese, Crab &
        Tomatoes 31

Tahitian Vanilla Shrimp 27
Servais, Tom 164, 247
Seven Sisters 168
Shackleton, Ernest 210
Shrimp
  Avocados Stuffed with Jumbo Shrimp 173
  Citrus Shrimp & Salmon Ceviche 229
  Mushrooms & Shrimp (Zurrukatuna) 43
  Peruvian Quinoa-Honey Shrimp 233
  Shrimp Phyllo Purses with Tomato
      Chermoula Sauce 116
  Spicy-Sweet Shrimp & Eggplant Soup
      (Terung Lodeh) 210
  Tahitian Vanilla Shrimp 27
Shrimp Phyllo Purses with Tomato
    Chermoula Sauce 116
Slater, Kelly 98, 138, 192, 247
Smith, Jordy 23
Smoky Corn Salsa 105
Smoothies
Bethany's Açai Smoothie 139
Bethany's Papaya Nut Smoothie 139
  Snapper in Ti Leaves with Spinach &
      Orange-Ginger Sauce 34
Society Islands 14, 26
Solomon 108
Sonoma 79
Souk 118
Soup
  Crab Bisque 48
  Marrakesh Butternut Squash Soup 112
  Pozole 162
  Salvadoran Seafood Soup (Mariscada) 95
  Spicy-Sweet Shrimp & Eggplant Soup
      (Terung Lodeh) 210
Soup Bowls 192
soup contests 48-49
Spain 40, 44, 58, 60, 61, 191
Spicy-Sweet Fruit Salad (Rujak) 209
Spicy-Sweet Shrimp & Eggplant Soup 210
St. Ann Parish 180
St. Barts 188
St. George, Barry 184
St. Thomas 186
Steamed Chile-Ginger Halibut 214
Stone, Jamie 69
Strauch, Paul 153
Stuffed Yams with Cheese, Crab &
    Tomatoes 31
Sumatra 12, 212, 215
Sumbawa 215
summer rolls 203
Sunn, Rell 21, 32, 142, 143
Sunn, Rell 32, 142-143
Sunset Beach 153

Surfer magazine 6, 18, 103, 248
Surfer's Choice teriyaki sauce 70
Surfwise Steel-Cut Oatmeal 86
Sweet Chile Sauce 214
sweet potatoes 189
tacos 154, 156, 169, 170
Taghazout 110, 115
Tahiti 14, 26, 30, 151
Tahitian Vanilla Shrimp 27
Taiwan 16
Takayama, Donald 70, 71
Talafofo Bay 18
Tamarind Olive Sauce 183
Tamarindo 92
Tamni 114
Tangier 112
Tapas 40, 44, 60
Tavarua 22, 23, 25, 164
Tavarua Surf Camp Banana Bread 23
tequila 66, 67, 170, 171
Terung Lodeh 210
Thompson, Ann 192
Thundercloud Reef 22
Ti Punch Rum Cocktail 186
Tijuana 7, 66, 156, 164
Timor 208
Tobago 184, 185, 190
Todos Santos Island 170
Toiny Coast 188
Tomato Chermoula Sauce 117
Tomson, Michael 22
Tomson, Shaun 160
Tracks magazine 42
Trattoria Don Angelo 231
Trent, Buzzy 153
Trinidad 183, 190, 196
Trinidad Coleslaw 190
Tropic of Cancer 16
Tropic of Capricorn 16
Trujillo 220
Tuamotu 20
Tuareg Berbers 112, 122-123
Tudor, Joel 70
Tumon Bay 34
Tuna Steaks with Onion Marmalade 54
Turkey, Kalua 143
Turks 182, 183, 189, 190
Turtle Bay 150, 248
Uluwatu 208
Van Dyke, Jost 186
Vegan
  Agadir Almond Crunch 119
  Alto Pico Salad 231
  Cousinat (Vegetable Casserole, omit
      ham) 57

Killer Seven-Vegetable Tagine 111
Roasted Vegetables with Caramelized
    Balsamic Glaze 75
Salad Taghazout (omit the cheese) 115
Santo Domingo Sweet Potatoes with
    Pineapple-Rum-Balsamic Glaze 189
Spicy-Sweet Fruit Salad (Rujak) 209
Vegetable dishes
  Blanched Vegetables in Peanut Sauce
      (Gado Gado) 216
  Cousinat (Vegetable Casserole) 57
  Grilled Fish & Vegetable Packet 70
  Killer Seven-Vegetable Tagine 111
  Marrakesh Butternut Squash Soup 112
  Pancit Pohnepei (noodles with
      vegetables) 17
  Roasted Vegetables with Caramelized
      Balsamic Glaze 75
  Santo Domingo Sweet Potatoes with
      Pineapple-Rum-Balsamic Glaze 189
Vegetarian
  Agadir Almond Crunch 119
  Alto Pico Salad 231
  Cousinat (Vegetable Casserole, omit
      ham) 57
  Doña Victoria's Kahlúa Coconut
      Flan, 174
  Gado Gado (omit shrimp paste) 216
  Killer Seven-Vegetable Tagine 111
  Palauan Papaya Upside-Down Cake 28
  Roasted Vegetables with Caramelized
      Balsamic Glaze 75
  Salad Bar 146-147
  Salad Taghazout 115
  Santo Domingo Sweet Potatoes with
      Pineapple-Rum-Balsamic Glaze 189
  Spicy-Sweet Fruit Salad (Rujak) 209
Velzy, Dale 72, 73, 247
Velzyland 72
Viertel, Peter 53
Vietnam 16
Viti Levu 22
Waikiki 18, 142, 144, 146, 153, 222,
    224, 248
Waimea Bay 10, 18, 150
Walsh, Ian 138
Wayne, John 226
Wilson, Julian 98
Witzig, John 42
Yams with Cheese, Crab & Tomatoes 31
Yap 25, 28, 29
yellowtail 33, 34
Zihuatanejo 172
Zurrukatuna (Mushrooms & Shrimp) 43

Acknowledgments

Nothing could have been more of a pleasure than working with the characters who provided content for this book. The array of talent in these pages spans a lifetime of world adventure. There are many people to thank, so let me start with the most involved:

I owe the success of this book to Bill Schildge, my collaborator on this project. Bill is a master of many photographic genres: concerts, architecture, business, and action sports. Little did I know when he offered to help that he'd be a genius at food photography as well. I know of no one who takes more pride, has more ideas, or is easier to work with. Apologies, Bill, for any weight gained while chowing on our subjects.

Jeff Divine, my good friend for life, knew just what was needed to illustrate this book. For thirty years we have surfed and traveled the world together.

Tom Servais, whose backgammon skills are eclipsed only by his photographic gifts, was a major contributor, and part of a trio with Divine and me at *Surfer* back in the day.

Art Brewer was the third master photographer from the *Surfer* stable. He is a virtuoso colorist and an astute observer who fills an image with inflection, personality, and mood.

More amazing images came from other talented shooters who helped with particular locations or subjects: Brent Schlea, Pierre Gascogne, Brian Bielmann, Guy Motil, and Aurelien Laborde.

For location shoots and outstanding photo styling, a huge shout-out to Mary Landis at the Arrañaga Beach Road home. Thanks as well to Michael and Leslie Davis and Bob and Pat Hasbrook, who opened their kitchens and their hospitality, as they have so many times before.

To my favorite dining companion, Steve Pezman, and my favorite surf-soaked celebrity chef, Raphael Lunetta, a huge debt of gratitude for their wonderful forewords.

I'm grateful for David Rensin, friend and writer extraordinaire, who helped shape the book proposal. Bob Yehling earns a thank you for getting me to write the first twenty stories. And thanks to Dale Velzy, Greg Long, Steve Barilotti, and Joe and Teasha Curren for letting me share stories from their travels. *Vaya con dios*, fellow travelers.

Thanks to Suzy Evans, my fabulous literary agent from Dijkstra Literary Agency, who saw the vision and took it to the publishing world. I never had anyone return a cold call as fast as she did—we must be destined for more books!

Martin Daley provided incredible travel opportunities while I worked on the Quiksilver Crossing Project. Thanks to Bethany Hamilton and her entire *ohana*, Caliche Alfaro, Victoria Dones, Duncan Campbell, Kelly Slater, Laird Hamilton, and Denny Doyle, who all shared favorite dishes with me.

Cass Husted, Randy Rarick, Vicki Patterson, Jodi Wilmott, Mike Muir, Shannon North, Victoria Calhoun, Bob McKnight, Cathey Curtis, Randy Hild, Tim Meek, and Bruce Vogen—thank you for inspiration and assistance.

To Prospect Park Books and my tireless editor and publisher, Colleen Dunn Bates, who grew up on

Beach Road and believed in the book from the beginning, thank you for putting up with me and giving me an amazing product. Thanks as well to her crew: Dorie Bailey, Caitlin Ek, editors Pat Jalbert-Levine and Leilah Bernstein, publicist Trina Kaye, and designers Amy Inouye, and Michelle Ingram.

For their assistance and support both on the book and over the years, thanks to Joey and Yana Cabell and the Waikiki Chart House, Turtle Bay Resort, Ryan and Julie at Witch's Rock Surf Camp, Miguel Vegas van Oordt and the Chicama Boutique Surf Hotel, Sean Murphy at Waterways, Oliver Fitzjones and Dan Haylock of Stormrider Publications, Henry Morales and the Los Flores Surf Resort, Dave Gilovich and Marcus Sanders at Surfline, Todd and Pete Taras at *Surfer* magazine, Mace Hulet, Sean Pezman, and the whole crew at *The Surfer's Journal,* and most of all to my family, Jann, Kim, Sam, and James. And to a million people I appreciate but am overlooking.

About the Author

Jim Kempton has spent his professional and personal life in the surf world. A lifelong traveler who was born on Guam and has visited and/or lived in more than thirty countries, Jim has been editor and publisher of *Surfer* magazine, group publisher for TransWorld Publishing, media director at Billabong USA, and director of Quiksilver Crossing. He also founded and ran the former Margarita's Village, a regional Mexican restaurant in San Clemente, California.

Jim is currently president of the California Surf Museum, a contributor to national and international surfing publications, and a surf-industry consultant. He also serves on the Surfrider Foundation Advisory Board, and the Sport of Kings Foundation. His other books include *Surfing: The Manual* and *The San Onofre Surfing Club.*

A graduate of United States International University, Jim holds an MBA in international business. He lives in San Clemente with his wife, Jann, and their three children live nearby. And Jim still surfs.